Side by Side

Being Christian in a Multifaith World

R I C H A R D   P.   O L S O N

Foreword by Charles Kimball

JUDSON PRESS
PUBLISHERS SINCE 1824
VALLEY FORGE, PA

Side by Side: Being Christian in a Multifaith World
© 2018 by Judson Press, Valley Forge, PA 19482-0851
All rights reserved.

The author and Judson Press have made every effort to trace the ownership of all quotes. In the event of a question arising from the use of a quote, we regret any error made and will be pleased to make the necessary correction in future printings and editions of this book.

Bible quotations in this volume are from the New Revised Standard Version Bible, copyright© 1989, Division of Christian Education of the National Council of the Churches of Christ in the United States of America. Used by permission. All rights reserved.

Scripture quotations marked Phillips are from The New Testament in Modern English, Rev. Ed. Copyright © J.B. Phillips 1972. Used by permission of The Macmillan Company and Geoffrey Bles, Ltd.

Library of Congress Cataloging-in-Publication data
Names: Olson, Richard P., author. Title: Side by side : being Christian in a multifaith world/Richard P. Olson. Description: First [edition].|Valley Forge: Judson Press, 2018.|Includes bibliographical references. Identifiers: LCCN 2017025704 |ISBN 9780817017903 (pbk.: alk. paper) Subjects: LCSH: Christianity and other religions—United States.|Christianity and culture—United States. Classification: LCC BR526 .O58 2018 | DDC 261.2—dc23 LC record available at https://lccn.loc.gov/2017025704

Printed in the U.S.A.
First printing, 2018.

Contents

Foreword by Charles Kimball   iv

Introduction: My Journey   viii

1. Moving beyond Boredom to Encounter   1

2. A Similar Search, Shared Spiritual Practices   13

3. God Is One; God Is Not One   27

4. Conversation or Conversion?   40

5. Evil Religions, or Evil Possibilities in Each Religion   59

6. We All Have Reasons to Repent   71

7. Questions, Critiques, and Misunderstandings   89

8. Building Understanding by Serving Side by Side   102

9. The Ultimate Questions   112

10. A Christlike Presence among the "Nones"   125

11. Shared Life with Fellow Christians Who Disagree with Me   140

12. Where Does This Lead Us?   151

Bibliography   167

FOREWORD

Sir Francis Bacon (1561–1626), English author and philosopher, famously proffered this reflection on books: "Some books are to be tasted, others to be swallowed, and some few to be chewed and digested: that is, some books are to be read only in parts, other to be read but not curiously, and some few to be read wholly, and with diligence and attention." In my view, Richard Olson's book Side by Side: Being Christian in a Multifaith World meets the criteria for inclusion on the list of a rare "few to be chewed and digested. " It is a timely, engaging, and accessible book that needs to be discussed, debated, and utilized "with diligence and attention." This bold claim and affirmation deserves explanation. Why is this book so important and timely?

The world today is vastly different from previous eras. We live in an increasingly interconnected and interdependent world community. As the title of Olson's book suggests, we now live Side by Side with an astonishing diversity of people who embrace different religious convictions and worldviews. The global dynamics visible in daily headlines are now present at the national and local levels as well. The extensive research of Harvard professor Diana Eck's Pluralism Project reveals how the United States is now the most religiously diverse country in the world. And, the diversity is not found simply in large cities such as New York, Los Angeles, Chicago, and Houston. Today, every U.S. city with a population of 100,000 or more is literally a microcosm of the world community with Jews, Christians, Muslims, Hindus, Buddhists, Taoists, practitioners of Shinto and of various indigenous traditions living side by side.

The twenty-first century may well be defined by interfaith relationships. The ways in which people of faith relate to one another in local, national, and international settings present both great challenges and great opportunities. The status of Jewish-Christian-Muslim rela-tions—the focus of Olson's book—presents a mixed and precarious dynamic. One can point to substantial improvements in Jewish-Chris-tian relations since World War II, but these are set against a backdrop of a long and deplorable history of Christian anti-Semitism. And, as large white supremacist rallies (such as the now infamous one in 2017 in Charlottesville, Virginia, where the torch-bearing mob chanted "Jews will not replace us!"), threats against Jewish institutions, and the desecration of Jewish cemeteries make plain, anti-Semitism re-mains a very present reality.

Similarly, we can identify a number of constructive initiatives for education and cooperation among Christians and Muslims in recent decades. Even so, persistent Islamophobia and misunderstandings about the basics of Islam are widespread in the West. Understand-able media focus on horrific actions by violent extremists who claim inspiration from Islam provides fuel for many politicians, pundits, and preachers to fan the flames of fear about the world's second largest religion.

There are no easy answers or simple solutions to the multiple chal-lenges presented by interfaith relationships. But the way forward is not blocked. Olson's thoughtful and accessible book makes enor-mously valuable contributions at this point, especially for individuals and local congregations. He not only illustrates the pragmatic neces-sity of peaceful coexistence; he underscores how respectful under-standing and cooperation with neighbors is central for followers of Jesus. The apostle Paul's admonition states it clearly: "Insofar as it is possible with you, live peaceably with everyone" (Romans 12:18).

But why is this directive so difficult to fulfill? A history of misun-derstanding, fears of the "other," and periods of conflict present major obstacles. Even more, longstanding theological presuppositions con-tinue to block many faithful Christians from intentionally pursuing constructive relationships with Jewish and Muslim neighbors. The subtitle of the book—Being Christian in a Multifaith World—prepares the reader to explore the often vexing theological issues of particularity and pluralism while discovering specific ways to live faithfully alongside people of different religions. In each chapter Olson provides substantial food for thought, inviting diligent readers and discussion groups to chew and digest.

The autobiographical framework for the book is both appropriate and effective. Readers are invited to discover what Dick Olson has discovered over many years. His faith journey is rooted in his American Baptist tradition but takes him into the wider world of Christian ecumenism and finally interfaith explorations. A large segment of Christian readers will easily identify with his experiences and the questions he formulates along the way. Olson continually wrestles with the overriding question: How can one be a person of deep and committed faith while also acknowledging that one's own experiences and theological framework do not exhaust all the possibilities within and beyond the Christian tradition?

He gently but clearly shares ways he has grown, learned, and changed over time. He does this as a pastor and teacher who wants readers to come to their own conclusions as they explore anew what the teachings of Jesus and other parts of the Bible might reveal to our time and circumstances. Accordingly, he includes helpful and provocative questions and suggestions for consideration at the end of each chapter in a section labeled "Reflect, Discuss, Do."

Seminarians will find Side by Side to be invaluable as they train for vocations in Christian ministry. Clergy will appreciate the guidance and access to useful resources; many will find a wealth of material for sermons or series of sermons. Individuals and adult study groups will discover a great deal about their theological presuppositions and options for specific ways to learn, grow, and work together with Jews, Muslims, and others for the betterment of their communities.

Christian readers will not all come to the same conclusions—especially theologically—on how to formulate a faithful approach to particularity and pluralism. Olson not only recognizes this; he affirms it. At several key points he offers his view or an image that he finds instructive. He then invites the reader to embrace that view or image if it is helpful; if not, then leave it. Throughout, however, he affirms both the mandate to overcome inaccuracies and misunderstandings about other religions and the responsibility to live peaceably with others.

Thirty years ago I completed my doctoral dissertation at Harvard Divinity School focusing on what had been learned during the first twenty years of Christian-Muslim Dialogue programs convened by Protestant and Orthodox Christians through the World Council of Churches and the Roman Catholic Church after Vatican II. As a Baptist minister and student of world religions with specialization in Islam and Jewish-Christian-Muslim relations, I have lectured and spoken in several hundred colleges, universities, churches, synagogues, and mosques. I have also been an active participant in interfaith programs at every level. I know from experience that large numbers of Christians recognize the importance of positive interfaith relationships and are eager to facilitate these relations. In this valuable volume, Dick Olson has provided a treasure chest of information that builds upon what people of faith and goodwill have done, even as it equips individuals and congregations to lead constructive interfaith initiatives in our interdependent, interconnected, and all too quarrelsome world of the twenty-first century.

Charles Kimball
Professor and Chair, Religious Studies Department
The University of Oklahoma

INTRODUCTION
My Journey

I thank my God every time I remember you, constantly praying with joy in every one of my prayers for all of you.
—Philippians 1:3

In a few decades, the United States has changed from a largely Christian nation to the most religiously diverse nation in the world. It is so important that we as Christians understand this, engage it, and respond to it in ways pleasing to our Lord. This book will explore how to think and act in this new era of history, but first I will tell you about the personal journey that brings me to this discussion.

My Denominational Family

My birth and growth as a Christian has been influenced and enriched by two communities.

One of these was my denominational family. I was the second child of Ole and Hazel Olson, American Baptist home missionaries serving isolated rural churches on the plains of South Dakota. My father had been born on a homestead in the Dakota territory to Norwegian immigrant parents and was raised and schooled Lutheran. Out of study and conversations with friends, he became a convinced Baptist and eventually a much-loved pastor.

Our home was graced by love, prayer, Bible study, and much church activity. My sister, Ruth, and I sometimes attended as many as three Vacation Bible Schools a summer as we participated in our parents' ministry outreach. I was baptized by my dad at a very young age, after being a part of his baptismal classes with at least two groups of older boys. I remember my excitement and joy at that outdoor service on a beautiful July day. Baptisms were done in a little pond on a farm owned by one of the families in the church.

My father's untimely death when I was nine years old was devastating for our family and our little church. Ironically, for me it was also a time of discovery. As we mourned and remembered together, I saw, even at that young age, what he meant to those touched by his ministry. I trace the beginning of my sensing a call to ministry from that time of reflection after his death.

In the years following, my home church and the wider denomination were lifelines for my family and me. Sunday morning worship, choir practice, and Baptist Youth Fellowship (young people made up more than half of our church) marked the rhythms of our weeks. Although poor in material things, we were rich in love and caring. Kindly older church members affirmed us, encouraged our growth as Christians and leaders, fed us, and welcomed us into their homes. As I grew in my awareness of a call to ministry, I was often mentored by my home pastor, Jeannie Sherman.

The annual state youth conventions and the much-anticipated summer youth camp at Camp Judson in the beautiful Black Hills were social and spiritual highs. Singing rounds around the tables, taking quick dips in icy Rapid Creek, hearing inspiring stories of faith and service around a campfire on chilly evenings under a star-filled sky— all this "recharged my batteries," so to speak. I met, dated, and eventually married one of the beautiful young women from another church youth group that participated in these activities.

As the years went on, my church helped me financially to attend our area's Baptist college as well as a Baptist seminary in the east. In both places, I enjoyed the intellectual challenge of exploring the depths of the faith, and experienced many moments of inspiration. My friends along the way—sometimes thoughtful, sometimes zany— added joy and warmth to my growth and discovery.

Finally that glorious day came when I returned to my home church and stood before an ordination council to present and defend my statement of faith and beliefs. After lively discussion and a positive vote, I was ordained in my home church. It was a great day, both for me and for that congregation, which had struggled to stay alive through the drought and depression of the 1930s. I was the first child of that parish to enter ordained ministry. They saw this event as an affirmation of their service throughout the years.

I then served as pastor for many years in various congregations before becoming a professor, teaching the next generation of ministers in yet another of our denominational seminaries, Central Baptist Theological Seminary. Some years were more joyous than others, but the bond of love within my spiritual family remained as we studied Scripture, worshipped God, cared for each other in our joys and griefs, and sought to serve the world as part of God's wider family.

In 1996, when one church I was serving granted me a three-month sabbatical, I had the privilege of being a short-term missionary, offering retreats, training, and educational events in Indonesia, Thailand, and Myanmar (Burma). I returned feeling renewed and revived by the wonderful friendships I developed with those who were serving so faithfully in much less hospitable places to Christianity than where I lived.

I gratefully embrace my heritage as a Christian, even while my Baptist denomination, along with many others, is experiencing so much transition and change.

Ecumenical Experiences

The second community that has enriched my spiritual growth is the ecumenical body of believers and, in time, the interfaith community. While my denomination means much to me, we are a tiny part of the larger believing world. Led by my American Baptist leaders, I have embraced this reality and entered into the broader community of believers.

I remember the comment some years ago by our General Secretary at the time, Edwin Tuller. When asked why American Baptist Churches USA was part of the then-controversial World Council of Churches, he responded that we don't approve of every action taken by the WCC but wanted to add our voice and to vote on such measures. He added (and I am quoting from memory), "We are also there to learn from others and to teach others what we treasure in the richness of our Christian heritage and perspective."

Following his leadership, I have engaged in many ecumenical opportunities in the communities where I served. Even more, I have found enrichment and mutual strengthening in the informal friendships with my fellow clergy in these other denominations. I remember one time when I experienced such support, even though I was unaware of it at the time. In the church where I served as pastor, a couple disliked me and disapproved of my perspective. They had two sons. One afternoon, their younger son, who was junior-high age, was killed when a car struck his bicycle. Whatever our interpersonal differences, I was their minister. I called on them, spent time with them, offered what solace I could, and prepared for the memorial service. I dreaded conducting that funeral, but to my amazement, the service went much better than I had imagined possible. I felt upheld and strengthened as I led worship and comforted these grieving parents.

A day or two later, I learned that the three-person ministerial staff of the Presbyterian church across courthouse square from my church had known of the tragedy—and of my difficult relationship with the family. They had met together in prayer, upholding me for the entire time of that funeral. *That* was the source of my unexpected strength.

Experiences such as this remind me that, as much as I love my own denomination, the Christian family is much, much wider. It's easier to connect with some denominations than others, but I have always had pastoral friendships where we would help each other out and back each other up when needed. Relating to most of my Protestant larger family has been spontaneous and fairly easy.

Relating to Roman Catholics has not always been as easy for us Protestants. Thankfully, tensions have lessened and changed in recent years. As I look back, I now realize what a gift Father Thomas Healy was to me. I met this Catholic priest in the 1940s during the last years of my father's ministry and life. In our previous community, the relationship with Catholics, and particularly the priest, had been extremely strained. That priest would cross the street to avoid talking to a Baptist minister. Sadly, such tensions were widespread. Ethnicity and religion intertwined in many communities. Catholics and Protestants kept to themselves, did as little commerce as possible with the other (sometimes even boycotting the other's businesses), and forbade their children to date or marry persons of the "other religion."

Given that atmosphere, my parents were surprised to be told that in Timber Lake, our next home community, the priest was the custodian of the keys to the rental house we would occupy. When we arrived, my dad knocked on the priest's door to get those keys. A gracious, elderly Irish priest greeted him warmly and invited our family in. He served my parents tea and offered cookies to Ruth and me.

That was the beginning of a warm friendship between Father Healy and my dad. From time to time, Father Healy would come over for an evening of chess with Dad. He would bring his fancy chess set, and they would laugh and enjoy each other as they played.

On the morning that my dad died, Father Healy, whose house was just down the street from us, saw all the activity and called us to find out what was happening. When my mother told him that Dad had died, Father Healy came over to our house immediately. One of the first callers, he pressed some money into my mother's hand.

His friendship continued with our next minister, as much as the practices of the Roman Catholic church allowed. He once accepted her invitation to speak to our youth group about his trip to Ireland. When our church caught on fire one Easter morning, he made his church building available to us for our Easter service after their Mass was over. He even offered extended use of their building for our worship services while we rebuilt, although our congregation chose another building instead. (We actually met in the basement of the pool hall, owned by one of our church members.)

Still, the harsh social distinctions and regulations between the two religious groups remained. Any non-Catholic marrying a Catholic had to sign an agreement that their children would be raised Catholic in order for the Catholic member to stay in the good graces of the church. Moreover, the non-Catholic spouse was urged to convert. One girl from our youth group who married a Catholic man chose to convert and had to confess regret about her years of "error" as a Protestant. Indeed, Protestants were described as "schismatics and heretics." While the decency and kindness of priests like Father Healy could soften that a bit, they couldn't eliminate it. In a time of such difficult church policies, Father Healy and my father were my first examples of what it means to be Christlike in an interreligious and often conflicting world.

This atmosphere changed in the 1960s when Pope John XXIII called the Second Vatican Council. He said it was time to open the windows of the church and let in some fresh air, and he invited other Christian bodies to send internal observers—an invitation accepted by some Protestant and Eastern Orthodox groups. For non-Catholic Christians, he replaced the older term of "schismatics and heretics" with "separated brothers." In the parlance of the day, he did not add "and sisters," although in my experience it was his "sisters," the women religious in the Roman Catholic church, who opened the windows most widely to service in the world and fellowship with Christians of other traditions.

I was a pastor in a small city in Wisconsin during this time. The nuns at St. Joseph Hospital, who had always been kind and helpful to the Protestant ministers who visited their congregants at the hospital, were most eager to claim the new freedoms of Vatican II. They seemed to claim this freedom in many ways.

When allowed, almost immediately these nuns planned an ecumenical prayer retreat and invited several of us, their Protestant minister friends, to share reflections or guided prayer times. It was a rich day of initiating and developing a deeper fellowship and trust. The day ended with Mass, and in accordance with the practice that has continued to the present, the non-Catholics were not allowed to receive the sacrament of the Eucharist. For some, this has been a stumbling block to interdenominational relations. At times I have felt that barrier, but at other times I've sensed our deep and growing oneness despite the restriction.

I remember once such moment. As part of a study time in Israel in 2009, my group was spending a week at the Tantur Ecumenical Institute, located between Jerusalem and Bethlehem. On one of our free evenings I chose to attend a Roman Catholic Mass, along with half a dozen other Protestants in our group. When we rose to go forward for the Eucharist, we approached the priest respectfully, with our arms folded across our chests to request a blessing, as was the protocol. The officiant that evening was a priest from Nigeria. When I approached the altar, he held out his arms and embraced me warmly and whispered such a caring blessing that I could not have felt more loved by God, sacrament or not. In our remaining days at Tantur, when he would see me at the evening meal, he would come over to greet me and we would spend a few moments together.

Over the years, relationships between Catholics and non-Catholics have changed, grown, and increased considerably. Marriage regulations as to which clergy must officiate, where the wedding can be, and what promises are to be made have moderated. Mutual learning and enrichment now occur on many levels. For example, at the seminary where I taught, our president, Rev. Dr. Molly Marshall, led us into a significant relationship with the community of Benedictine monks at Conception Abbey in Missouri. Faculty retreats and student orientations often happen there now, and from time to time Dr. Marshall herself conducts a course on Benedictine spirituality and hospitality that includes a week's residence at the abbey, in which students enter into the daily rhythm of chanting the psalms and praying together.

Ecumenical relationships worldwide have improved significantly over the years. The changes I have seen in my lifetime are a parable of hope for me. As we live in this age of rapid change, we must consider how to live out and strengthen these deepened relationships among Christians in the days ahead. If Catholics and Protestants can overcome ancient barriers, learning from one another and developing deeper bonds of fellowship, we may experience unimagined results in our interfaith relationships.

Interfaith Explorations

In reflecting back on my experiences with interfaith relationships, I must acknowledge that, while I am interested in deeper understanding among all the world's religions, I have the most experience and feel the most urgency in the relationship among the three Abrahamic religions: Judaism, Christianity, and Islam. This is where I will concentrate my attention in this book.

Though I took a seminary course in contemporary Judaism from Rabbi Albert Gordon, a notable sociologist, for most of the years of my ministry, my contact with the Jewish community was minimal and infrequent. At the same time, movies and books about the Holocaust have deeply moved and disturbed me. When the United States Holocaust Memorial Museum advertised a week of study for a select group of seminary and college professors on the theme "Christianity and the Holocaust: Asking the Hard Questions," my seminary nominated me. I was selected to be part of the interfaith group of fifteen scholars who explored these hard questions. We considered some little-known, painful aspects of Christian history that influenced the various steps that led to the Holocaust. I will tell you more about that in chapter six.

One of the expectations for participants was that we use our learnings in some way in our educational work. Several of my colleagues in that group already taught courses on Judaism, Holocaust studies, or comparative religion. I did not teach any classes of this sort, so I decided to prepare a general lecture for my seminary as well as put together a series of sessions to share with congregations, Christian or Jewish, when invited to speak. In my preparation, I could not escape the question: what does this call forth from me?

At about the same time, Rabbi Alan Cohen, who had just retired from a local conservative synagogue, contacted me. He was using his retirement years to create an interfaith clergy group and asked me to serve on his board. I eagerly agreed, and our subsequent work together and the events we designed and experienced broadened my believing world.

My deepening relationship with persons in the Islamic community also came as the result of an assignment to chair a committee to plan a Muslim-Baptist event. Before that, I was aware of the fear and hysteria about Muslims in the wake of 9/11 and other terrorist attacks. Somehow this did not square with the times of devout prayers in mosques I observed during a trip to Egypt, nor with what I saw in the Muslim nation of Indonesia while on my sabbatical. I knew only a few American Muslims, most of them professionals providing valuable services in the medical field and others.

I was at a loss how to proceed when a challenge came my way. In 2007, a large group of Islamic scholars wrote or signed off on a document sent to the major Christian bodies of the world. Entitled "A Common Word," it was an invitation to dialogue around the two great commandments: love God, and love your neighbor.[1] Various religious bodies, including the Baptist World Alliance, responded in turn with conferences, conversations, and documents. American Baptists held a dialogue event with Islamic scholars at Andover Newton Theological School in Newton, MA. Afterwards, denominational leaders felt this discussion should be extended to more persons in other parts of the country.

The seminary where I taught, Central Baptist Theological Seminary, was asked to create such an event in the Midwest, and we were provided a modest fund to help make it happen. My seminary president asked me to chair the Muslim-Baptist dialogue event. I was to recruit prospective members for a planning committee and develop the committee's fellowship and trust so that they could effectively plan and facilitate the event. The only stipulation was that both Muslims and Baptists needed to be on this planning committee.

And so began my adventure of searching for both Muslims and Baptists to serve on the planning committee. I found suggestions for possible committee members, talked to them, and persuaded them to participate. We discovered that our best meeting time was after work and before evening schedules, so we decided to have dinner together as we talked. By so doing, we learned what foods were appropriate for all and which caterers could provide food that met our joint requirements. Our meeting schedule also included time for Isha, the sundown prayers of Muslims. So Shakil, one of our devout Muslim committee members, would excuse himself to go wash and find a private place to pray. (We learned that he used an app on his smartphone to enable him to face Mecca for his prayers!) Mahnaz, another Muslim member, chose to do her evening prayers a little later, at home, after our gathering.

A year and a half later, we held our Muslim-Baptist dialogue day. We began with a generous meal that all those present could enjoy, then continued with presentations and guided conversations, with Muslims and Christians at every table. More than one hundred Muslims and Christians who had never participated in such discussions before filled our large room.

I believe that event was very important in helping participants move into our larger believing world. However, I suspect even more significant was the deepened trust and friendship that developed among those of us who planned the event. It has certainly led me to further exploration, experiences, and growth, which I will discuss in this book as we proceed. Such moments of peace and growing mutual understanding are so significant in our troubled world. Coincidentally, we held our event shortly after the bombing at the Boston Marathon, so our discussions, poignant as they were, were much-needed and highly relevant.

The need for personal relationships with those of other faiths and a deeper understanding of one another's faith and heritage grows more urgent by the day. Persons commit vicious and violent acts, often claiming that their faith motivates them to do so. Suspicion of one another grows, and retaliation takes on various shapes and forms. Public policies are developed based on our worst suspicions of the other—policies about military engagement, immigration practices, and more. Persons with certain characteristics and suspected countries of origin are subjected to more restrictions and searches on airlines. Places of worship are vandalized. Students, even grade-school students, and workers are viewed with suspicion and possibly harassment when another public bombing or other attack occurs.

We all need to learn to think clearly about who is responsible for such events, and, even more importantly, who is not. We need to get to know one another, to form authentic relationships, to build the rudiments of trust. I seek to do so as a Christian, molded by Jesus' love for me and the world and striving to follow his example and teachings. As I read the Gospels anew, seeking to see Jesus in his own interreligious world—a brand new vantage point for me—I find passages jumping out at me, leading me to new insights. I now see Jesus teaching, healing, and providing food for people from wide geographical areas. He responded caringly to persons from other backgrounds, including a Roman centurion, a Canaanite woman, and a Samaritan woman—all from groups with long histories of political and religious conflict with Jews.

As we consider the fast-changing religious scene of our day, we will explore Christlike ways of relating and conversing with two other populations besides Jews and Muslims. One population includes the rapidly growing ranks of "spiritual-but-not-religious" or SBNRs, sometimes labeled the "Nones" (because of survey responses indicating no religious affiliation), the "Dones" (the church dropouts), and those who call themselves the "new atheists." The other population consists of the believing Christian community, who probably will disagree quite strongly with some of what I say in the following pages.

At the end of each chapter, I have provided a section entitled "Reflect, Discuss, Do" to encourage personal reflection, group conversation, and positive action.

It is unlikely that anyone, whatever one's roots and story, will agree with everything I say in this book. That is okay. I hope to stimulate reflection and conversation. Hang on, it's going to be quite a ride!

Reflect, Discuss, Do

1.What stories come to mind as you compare your journey with mine?

2. In what ways are you experiencing the multi-religious world?

3. Do you have friends or family from other Christian denominations? From other religions? What have you learned from them about interreligious relationships?

4. What questions do you have as we begin this journey? What do you hope to explore?

5. **Do:** Get acquainted with a person from another religion or a Christian denomination about which you have much to learn. Ask some questions.

Notes

1. The Royal Aal al-Bayt Institute for Islamic Thought, Jordan, "The ACW Letter / A Common Word between Us and You," October 13, 2007, accessed January 25, 2016, www.acommonword.com/the-acw-document/.

CHAPTER ONE

Moving beyond Boredom to Encounter

O mankind, We have indeed created you as male and female, and made you as nations and tribes that you might
come to know one another.
—Qur'an 49:13[1]

I sat in my study, unsure of where to start. I hoped the event would
go well, but I didn't know what to say.

My pastor and some church leaders had contacted the rabbi of the
synagogue that was our nearest neighbor, Congregation Ohev
Sholom. Our church leaders wanted to see what we could do to build
a deeper understanding between our two congregations of kindred
but differing faith traditions. It was agreed that a rabbi would conduct
a several-session introduction to Judaism at our church, and the synagogue would welcome a leader from our church for three Wednesday
evenings following their community meal.

My pastor recruited me, a seminary professor and retired pastor, to
present those programs. This was just before Lent, so when Ash
Wednesday would come, I would not spend it being anointed with
ashes, reminded of my mortality, and reflecting on Lent's holy mys-
teries with fellow Christians. Rather, I would be the guest of a Jewish
community as we sought deeper mutual understanding. When I asked
Rabbi Scott White what I should talk about, his response was general
and rather vague. He suggested presenting my Holocaust studies on
the second Wednesday. He was sure they would have questions from
our times together for the third Wednesday. For the first, I should

share whatever I wanted. But what did I want to share? That was the question that perplexed me as I stared at my blank computer screen. My mind went back to the first time I met people from their congregation, other than casual conversations with the rabbi and members at the annual interfaith Thanksgiving service.

At that time I was pastor of the church where I am now a member, and we were hosting the commencement exercises of our seminary on a Saturday morning in May. On that day we were being picketed by the infamous Westboro Baptist Church with their foul anti-gay signs and placards. As far as I could tell, this was in protest of the previous year's commencement speaker, whom they had inaccurately perceived as out-spokenly pro-gay. When the commencement service was over and we were enjoying refreshments together, one of the ushers came up to me and, with a quizzical look on his face, told me, "There are some people here who want to talk to the minister." I went to the adjoining room where two Jewish families awaited me. One of the fathers spoke for the group: "We're from Ohev Sholom. We saw the protesters, and we just want you to know we stand with you." "Thank you," I responded. "Perhaps I should tell you what that is about." He shook his head no, saying, "That doesn't matter. They're for hate. We just want you to know we stand with you." Each person shook my hand, and they left.

I decided to start with that recent story. But what would I say next?

I looked over my books and journals and browsed the Internet. I didn't find what I thought I should say, but I *did* find what *not* to say. My web browser pointed me to an article with a title something like "Why Interfaith Gatherings Bore Me." I no longer have the article, but I remember clearly what it said. Interfaith gatherings are boring, the author suggested, because people are so afraid of offending each other that they speak only in the blandest of generalities. That article hit home with me. I had experienced such services and gatherings. After the excitement of reaching out to one another, I left disappointed. It felt like we had done the polite, trivial exchanges people do before they truly get to know one another. We had stopped our discussion too soon, eaten our cookies, and gone home. I took that article to heart. I realized that my opening story would be okay, but if I stopped there, I would be equally guilty of avoiding true encounter through bland generalities.

When I met with the people at Ohev Sholom that first night, I acknowledged that we shared a heritage of Abraham and Moses, the psalms and the prophets. However, their forebears and mine had made different decisions about who Jesus was and what he means for the world. I reflected on the fact that our faith heritages have had pointed differences, some quite difficult, with each other. I told them that I came with the hope that, through open discussion of our differences as well as what we held in common, we could be part of deeper understanding. I also told them about my personal faith journey and what it means to me. Finally, I presented an overview of the variety in Christian denominations, the differences within my Baptist denomination in particular.

The second Wednesday, I shared my studies on Christianity and the Holocaust, as Rabbi White had requested. I dreaded that session because it felt like airing our "Christian dirty linen" about my forbears' prejudice and collusion in that awful history. (I should have realized they already knew that.) To my surprise, they found my presentation moving and appreciated my acknowledgment and grief at what happened.

This led to our third and concluding Wednesday together, when indeed those in attendance had plenty of questions and suggestions, and they acknowledged the differences and conflicts between our religious communities as well as the mutual respect and shared concerns. I think we parted friends, and everyone grew a little from the open conversations we had with one another.

A Sign of Hope

Since that experience, I have been hearing more and more advocacy for open sharing of one's beliefs and convictions in interfaith conversations and activities. The most recent example is found in an article I recently read about the Tri-Faith Initiative in Omaha, Nebraska.[2] After years of conversation, investigation, and planning, three faith groups—a Jewish synagogue, a Muslim mosque, and a Christian church—are building their places of worship, along with a fourth building for interfaith activities, on a common campus.

In addition to sharing their campus, the groups engage in a variety of activities together to get to know one another. They have a "robust children's program offering interfaith playtime for younger children and leadership development for teenagers." Furthermore, "the communities share meals together at public picnics and in each other's homes" as they learn how little they know about anyone's faith tradition but their own and begin to address that lack.[3]

The faith groups in this experiment have had to grapple with difficult questions such as the fact that their respective holy texts have passages that speak in disparaging ways of other faith groups. But they press on. Pastor and author Eric Elnes comments, "There's nothing more boring than an interfaith dialogue where everybody's just simply trying to be nice." Wendy Goldberg, a Tri-Faith Initiative board member, agrees and adds, "Most interfaith conversations are looking for places of sameness. In the Tri-Faith Initiative, we're looking to acknowledge that we are different, and that we cannot just tolerate but respect and trust and accept that there are other ways to know God."[4] They are aware of two other groups influenced by their experiment who are exploring a similar effort, one in Berlin and one in Arkansas.

I believe and hope we are moving into a new day of interfaith conversation. As these inspiring people show us, it is much more fruitful when persons of varying faith traditions deal forthrightly with our differences as well as our commonalities and what we can do together. I would hope that we would be free to tell each other not only the external details of our heritages but also how these faith traditions enrich our lives, touch our hearts, and transform us. As St. Irenaeus of Lyons said, "The glory of God is the human person fully alive."

Questions to Ask, Steps to Take

When we move beyond polite generalities to more genuine encounter, at least three questions emerge: (1) How should I relate to my neighbors of different faiths, and how do I initiate such conversations? (2)

How should I think about these neighbors and their beliefs and practices? (3) What impact does this have on me and my faith journey?

In this chapter, I will specifically explore the first of these and give a preliminary look at the second and third. Those questions will be explored in more depth in chapters to follow.

Religious Liberty

The place to begin is basic: to reaffirm the principle of religious liberty for all in our country—the right to believe and to practice the religion of one's choice. This also includes the right to choose not to practice any religion as well. This liberty is part of our American and our Christian DNA.

Religious liberty was pioneered by Roger Williams, who, in the 1600s, founded the Providence Plantation (which became the colony of Rhode Island) based upon principles of complete religious toleration, separation of church and state, and political democracy. Williams once said, "Forced worship stinks in God's nostrils."[5] This colony became a refuge for people persecuted for their religious beliefs. Anabaptists, Quakers, Jews, and Muslims settled in Rhode Island and were free to follow and live out their convictions. These principles continued for some hundred and fifty years and were reflected in the 1786 Virginia Statute for Religious Freedom, which in turn became the model for the first of ten amendments to the US Constitution—the Bill of Rights, adopted in 1791. The First Amendment states, "Congress shall make no law respecting an establishment of religion or prohibiting the free exercise thereof." While those who wrote this amendment addressed different issues of religious diversity than today, this principle stands as a trustworthy guide. We who want to worship and serve (or not) according to the dictates of our consciences should grant to others what we want for ourselves.

Intentional, Respectful Dialogue

Commitment to religious freedom is an important foundation, but it is equally important to build on that foundation. Intentional dialogue is an important way to start that process of building. As a guide designed by the World Council of Churches puts it:

> It is Christian faith in the Triune God . . . which calls us Christians to human relationship with our many neighbours. Such relationship includes dialogue: witnessing to our deepest convictions and listening to those of our neighbours. It is Christian faith which sets us free to be open to the faiths of others, to risk, to trust and to be vulnerable. In dialogue, conviction and openness are held in balance.[6]

I'd like to offer a few thoughts about carrying on such a dialogue for those who choose to do so. Every community has its unique challenges and opportunities, so perhaps not all of what I describe here fits what you or your group need. Feel free to select, choose, and follow your leading.

Such dialogue may be informal times with neighbors or meeting the parents of a child's classmates. Or the dialogue may be more formally designed, such as the synagogue-church and Muslim-Baptist conversations I've described. As a prologue to such conversations, it is important to learn the scope of the religious, cultural, and ideological diversity in our communities. Before we ask and look, this variety may be invisible to us.

As much as possible, it is wise for both (or all) faith groups to plan and lead interfaith events and conversations. These times might start with simple curiosity about the other and his or her world and progress to such questions as:

- What is your faith tradition?
- Do you have a local faith community in which you participate?
- What are the special holidays you celebrate in your tradition, and how do you observe them?
- What ceremonies do you have around rites of passage—births, initiation of children into your faith tradition, weddings, and death?

These are but examples of friendly door-openers to deeper discussions. Our Muslim-Baptist event began with a short quiz we created that provided questions around a few pieces of salient information known by one group or the other. It proved to be a helpful conversation starter.

Intentional Self-Definition

For conversations to grow, the advice of the World Council of Churches' document "Guidelines on Dialogue with People of Living Faiths and Ideologies" is crucial: "Partners in dialogue should be free to 'define themselves.' One of the functions of dialogue is to allow participants to describe and witness to their faith in their own terms. This is of primary importance since self-serving descriptions of other peoples' faith are one of the roots of prejudice, stereotyping, and condescension."[7]

Professor Todd Green approaches this from a slightly different angle in his book *The Fear of Islam: An Introduction to Islamophobia in the West*. Green defines Islamophobia as "hatred, hostility, and fear of Islam and Muslims and the discriminatory practices that result."[8] (This could, of course, be applied to tensions with other religious or ideological groups as well.) Green lists eight features of Islamophobia. For now, I will mention the first, which is to see Islam as monolithic and static. In Green's words:

> [This is the] notion that Islam lacks both diversity and internal differences and disagreements. In other words, all Muslims are basically the same, holding uniform world views and ide-ologies. . . . To put the matter starkly, if al-Qaeda [or ISIS] launches violent attacks against Western targets, some might conclude that this is due to an inherent quality in Islam, and that by extension all Muslims are fundamentally the same.[9]

A number of approaches to interfaith dialogue enable participants to define themselves on their own terms. I will suggest a few ways, but once the conversation flows, participants will discover others. One approach might be to ask each other: "What are the major varieties of practice and belief within your faith tradition, and where are you within this variety?" A follow-up question could be: "How do you define yourself within the diversity of your heritage?" Jews, for example, might respond by identifying Reform, Conservative, and Orthodox Judaism, and which one they embrace. Muslims might speak of the Sunni and Shiite branches and of other cultural varieties in the way their religion is practiced.

Another way to learn from each other might be to ask: "What has it been like as you have practiced your faith in the United States (or in this community)?" Religions have an impact on culture, and culture in turn has an impact on the religions within it. This is true for all faith traditions, but especially so for those who are minority groups. Responses might include experience from memories of earlier decades.

For examples, Jews might speak of restrictive housing areas up until the last few years, or the need to create their own "United Way" agency to offer care to the emergency and poverty needs of their community. Muslims might speak of the wide variety of cultures represented in their Islamic communities, persons from many parts of the world as well as a sizeable minority of African American members. They might also describe whether they or their children are harassed or welcomed in their communities. Possibly, the responses might focus on why they came to the United States and what makes them want to stay (or leave).

Or the responses might be from recent experiences and current headlines. For example, Jews in my community (Kansas City) might speak of the neo-Nazi who came into the city just two years ago, shooting persons going into the Jewish Community Center and the Shalom Retirement Community and killing three people. A Muslim family might tell (as one did at our dialogue event) of their junior-high son being harassed and bullied at school each time an al-Qaeda or ISIS terrorist attack occurred anywhere in the world.

All these possible discussions are meant to create an atmosphere where people of various faith heritages can hear the stories of others and be heard. Each person has an individual journey within that religion, and it is important to listen to each other's unique stories.

How Can We Know One Another Better?

When I was attempting to create community in the seminary classes where I taught, one of my ice-breaker questions was: "What about you, your faith tradition, and your faith journey do we need to know in order to really know you?" That question reveals the level of conversation to which we aspire. Perhaps this is a question that needs to be delayed when persons in the conversation come from different faith traditions. Still, this level of understanding and knowledge is a worthy goal of interfaith dialogue. It has happened and can happen again, I truly believe, when persons of goodwill speak openly about their distinct and varying perspectives.

Sharing food together may be a good strategy to start a dialogue experience or to celebrate at the end of a process. The experience of eating together and enjoying one another's presence and unique foods is a hospitable and tender way to experience what we have in common. At the same time, it will be important to know about dietary practices and regulations of the groups who will gather together: kosher for Jews, halal for Muslims. Any number of websites will describe what can be eaten and how it must be prepared. Local inquiry will easily reveal the restaurants or caterers that will prepare acceptable foods or provide recipes for your time together.

Preparing a dialogue event between two groups requires quite a time investment and openness to personal growth. Attendance may be smaller than hoped, and it will probably be the most open and adventurous persons from each of the groups who will attend. In other words, those who need it less will be there; those who need it most, likely will not. Nevertheless, it is important to make a start.

This planning group may want to include some further steps. One step may be educational and informational events in a less-threatening place, probably within each religion's own community. Public information events with a speaker offering an overview and history of another faith tradition might bring others into these conversations.

Another possibility to explore is some shared mission or community service project. Some people who are uneasy with talking may be open to working with persons of other traditions to build or repair a house, plant a community garden, or serve and clean up at a food kitchen for the homeless. We will speak more of this in chapter eight.

What Changes Might Happen?

I have shared some ideas on how to get the dialogue started. This brings us to the second set of questions: If I have truly and deeply entered into this dialogue, how do I respond to what I have heard? How should I think about my dialogue partners, their beliefs, rituals, and practices? What are my feelings? As much as possible, it is important to engage in this interfaith dialogue with an open heart and an open mind. What did I see to admire, or possibly to imitate? Also, what is strange or hard to understand and accept?

Changes can happen when dialogue occurs. I recall taking a multicultural class of students (including several African Americans) to a Friday evening Shabbat service at Congregation B'nai Jehuda, a Reform synagogue. This was a first-time experience for all the students. The service was in January, near Martin Luther King Day, and Rabbi Arthur Nemitoff spoke of King as one of God's prophets whose message was needed to address the economic injustices of the present day. The service concluded with the Cantor, Sharon Kohn, inviting us to join hands with those around us and sing "We Shall Overcome." After the service, we had an extended conversation with an informed layperson, a docent who responded to our questions about the worship we had experienced, about Judaism, and about the commitments of this congregation.

I saw the students change. Teachable but skeptical students began the evening wondering why we were doing this. Afterwards, they had a new view and different questions to ponder. Further, this is another possible way to answer the first question about how to initiate dialogue: attend each other's times of worship.

I remember another time when my wife and I attended a Sunday afternoon event at a local university. The theme was the Muslim experience in America. Though it was advertised as an interfaith event, very few non-Muslims were present. We felt a bit uneasy and out of place at the beginning. However, the atmosphere of the conference, the speakers, the literature provided, the tenor of the small-group conversations, and the hospitality and goodwill as we left made an impact on us. At the very least, we knew we would feel more relaxed at another such event. And we *would* attend another. It helped us move into ongoing dialogue, more willing to ask our hard questions and trust our partners in conversation.

This brings us to the third question that such dialogue raises: What impact has this dialogue had on me and on my faith journey? When I have met persons of integrity, generosity, and deep spirituality—persons formed by a faith tradition other than my own—what does this say to me? To what extent does it challenge my long-held beliefs and assumptions? In what ways might I feel called to change?

I have been doing much thinking, reading, discussing, and praying about these last two questions in recent months. In the following chapters, I will tell you what I am discovering and what is still in process for me. I invite you on this journey with me to whatever discoveries and conclusions each of us reaches and whatever commitments each of us will be called to make.

Reflect, Discuss, Do

1. When have you attended an ecumenical or interfaith event? What was your experience of the event? Was it boring and bland, with people speaking in generalities, or was it interesting and spirited, with a frank and lively exchange?

2. Which of the suggestions for growing in interfaith experience have you already undertaken? Which of the other suggestions intrigue and invite you?

3. Out of your experience, what are your thoughts about building interreligious conversations and understanding?

4. **Do:** Attend a worship experience of a religion other than your own. You may want to go with a small group. Call ahead and ask if visitors are welcome, when services are held, and what one should know before attending (special seating for non-members, appropriate

dress code, different expectations for women and men). It is possible that someone will offer to host you. Reflect with others about what you experienced.

Notes

1. Reza Shad-Kazemi, trans., "Introduction," *My Mercy Encompass All: The Koran's Teachings on Compassion, Peace and Love* (Berkeley: Counterpoint, 2007), 15.

2. Dawn Araujo-Hawkins, "A Jew, a Christian, and a Muslim walk into a parking lot…," *Sojourners*, June 2016, vol. 45, no. 6, 28–31.

3. Ibid.

4. Ibid.

5. Glenn W. LaFantasie, ed., *The Correspondence of Roger Williams, Volume II: 1654–1682* (Providence and London: Brown University Press/University Press of New England, 1988), 617–618, accessed January 4, 2016, http://www.worldpolicy.org/sites/default /files/uploaded/image/Williams-1670-Forced%20worship%20 stinks.pdf.

6. World Council of Churches, "Guidelines on Dialogue with People of Living Faiths and Ideologies," January 2, 2010, accessed July 15, 2016, https://www.oikoumene.org/en/resources/documents/wcc-programmes/interreligious-dialogue-and-cooperation/interreligious-trust-and-respect/guidelines-on-dialogue-with-people-of-living-faiths-a nd-ideologies.

7. Ibid.

8. Todd Green, *The Fear of Islam: An Introduction to Islamophobia in the West* (Minneapolis: Fortress Press, 2015), 9.

9. Ibid.

CHAPTER TWO

A Similar Search, Shared Spiritual Practices

My heart and my flesh sing for joy to the living God.
—Psalm 84:2b

You have made us for yourself, O Lord, and our hearts are
restless until they rest in you.
—Augustine of Hippo, *Confessions*

In this prayer, fourth-and fifth-century bishop Augustine of Hippo expressed a universal human longing that in some manner or other each
of us shares: we long for a deeper, closer relationship with the One
who is our source and our destiny. Many of us want to grow spiritually and to find ways to deepen our relationship with God. As we
search for places and practices to feed this hunger, we may be surprised at where this takes us, who is also there sharing the search, and
the practices that are helpful. As we explore our spiritual journeys,
two images about the interreligious world may be helpful.

In the 1970s, scholar Huston Smith wrote *The World's Religions:
Our Great Wisdom Tradition.* His master metaphor for the spirituality that religions share was a mountain and the view from the mountaintop. In Smith's understanding, it is this view and perspective that
all religions aspire to attain and where the deep, but often hidden,
oneness of various religions may be experienced. He wrote, "It is possible to climb life's mountain from any side, but when the top is

reached, the trails converge." Then he continued, "At base, in the foothills of theology, ritual, and organizational structure, the religions are distinct. Differences in culture, history, geography, and collective temperaments all make for diverse starting points."[1] But as one approaches the pinnacle of the mountain, views begin to converge. For those who reach the summit, a shared view of creation, the Creator, and of one another's religious pilgrimages becomes possible. This image helps illuminate the goal and purpose of most religions: to attain the unclouded view, to breathe the clear air, to find communion with the Divine One.

Another quite different image also points to this universal hunger and possibility. This image is expressed by Matthew Fox in his book *One River, Many Wells*.[2] In this book Fox builds on a quotation from the fourteenth-century Christian mystic Meister Eckhart: "God is a great underground river that no one can dam up and no one can stop."[3] One can take this metaphor in a variety of ways. For example, it is possible to apply this metaphor to denominations and religions, each a well. But if we taste one another's water, we discover we are drinking from the same source, the deep river that is God. Fox's application moves in a somewhat different direction. He explores a number of topics—such as joy, suffering, beauty, sacred sexuality, and dying—collecting views from the most spiritually insightful of many religions on each subject, going down to the river, so to speak. As he reveals the harmony and mutual enrichment among these varied heritages, he points to what he calls "Deep Ecumenism." This is where we share with one another our common and mutually enriching spiritual wisdom—the river.

While these metaphors speak to me, other people may find neither the mountain nor the river image all that helpful or reassuring. I was once asked to speak to a group of ministers of varying denominations who were volunteer chaplains for a hospital. The head chaplain wanted me to discuss how Christian clergy can minister with persons of other faith traditions. The conversation was going quite well until I suggested Fox's river image. At that moment, I promptly lost them. I suppose they thought I was asking them to forget the uniqueness of their Christian faith. In truth, all I was trying to say was that if we listen to a person of another faith on that person's terms, we might discover true spiritual friendship, with more in common than we might have anticipated. And that is what I am suggesting now.

If the image of a mountaintop view and/or the image of the subterranean river are helpful, embrace them; if not, leave them. For me they are an important starting point for us as Christians in an interreligious world. The initial understanding is this: the search of all peoples and all religions has a common starting point, one that unites us in the face of all that divides us in our various religions. That starting point is spirituality—our search and our practices.

We can explore where we are most deeply enriched spiritually within our own faith heritage. We can also learn from others of different religions what is spiritually enriching for them. We may discover some beliefs and experiences that we share, and quite possibly, we will learn much from one another. Let's take a look and see.

Starting on Common Ground

It is possible to find a number of places where people of various religions can meet spiritually. I remind you that we are concentrating on the three Abrahamic religions.

We all share an **awe for creation** and its many gifts. Each religion is guided by a **sacred text**. Engagement of that sacred text is a spiritual practice. Also, **devotional practices** are offered by each religion. Mutuality and learning are also found in the **mystical traditions** that seek communion with God. And we may come to our deepest appreciation of another religion when we meet spiritual persons of **integrity, ethics, hospitality, and compassion** in that faith tradition. By doing this exploration, we may not only discover interesting facts about the practices of others but also see our own spiritual quest in a new light.

Rabbi Lawrence Kushner offers some definitions that are a good place to start:

> Spirituality is religion experienced intimately. It's the core, the distilled essence of organized religion. Spirituality is where you and God meet—and what you do about it. . . . The late great mystical theologian Abraham Joshua Heschel once suggested that spirituality is life lived in the continuous presence of the divine.[4]

Kushner also reminds us that while we have much in common in our spiritual lives, each religion has distinctive aspects of spiritual practices. For example, while the very word *spiritual* seems to imply a split between the material world and the spiritual world, Judaism has no such distinction. There is only one world that is both material and spiritual.[5] In a similar vein, Hamza Andreas Tzortzis notes that Islam doesn't view spirituality separately from everyday activities.[6]

Shared Reverence and Encounter in Creation

Aware of our distinctions from one another, we also discover commonalities. For one, all three Abrahamic religions have a reverence, a sense of awe for creation, and our traditions all offer guidance on responsibility for stewardship of the earth.

Professor Emeritus Frederick M. Denny notes that in Islam God is the ultimate holder of dominion over creation, and that the Almighty gave humanity the trust (*amana*) for stewardship of creation. Creation itself is to be seen as a "sign" of God's power and majesty. Other living species are also considered by the Qur'an to be "peoples or communities" (*ummas*, Sura 6:38). The earth is mentioned 453 times in the Qur'an, with a strong sense of the goodness and purity of the earth. For example, clean dust may be used for ablutions before praying if clean water is unavailable. As Denny notes, the prophet Muhammed once said, "The earth has been created for me as a mosque and as a means of purification." Professor Denny points out that within these teachings is a profound awe of creation and the elements for a contemporary ecological ethic.[7]

Jews look to Genesis to affirm that the whole creation is the work and gift of God and then live in the light of that truth. To quote Rabbi Kushner again, "Everything in the world—trees, animals, oceans, stars, even people—conceals the One who made it and reveals the One who can be found inside it."[8] The presence of God in each created thing is there for those who take the time and effort to look and see.

The Hebrew Scriptures tell the story of how Jacob came to this awareness when he dreamed of a ladder joining heaven and earth. When he awoke he exclaimed, "Surely God was in this very place all along, and I didn't even know it!" (Genesis 28:16). Medieval French commentator Rabbi Shlomo Yitzchaki explained that what Jacob meant was, "If I had known God would be here, then I wouldn't have gone to sleep!"[9]

Christians share this heritage. We believe the creation is a gift of God, find God's presence within it, and have a growing sense of the deep and urgent need to care for the earth more responsibly. Christians have long believed that God provided two forms of revelation: Scripture and nature.

In April 1961 Soviet astronaut Yuri Gagarin had been the first to go into space and orbit the earth. While up there, he said, he looked for God, but he didn't see God anywhere, and therefore God didn't exist. Almost a year later, in February 1962, John Glenn was the first US astronaut to orbit the earth. After his successful return, a reporter asked him, "While up there, did you see God?" Glenn is said to have responded, "I never saw anything else." John Glenn articulated the spiritual awareness that all three religions (and others) share. Creation is a place to pay attention, to see and commune with God.

Spiritual Engagement of Sacred Texts

Each of the Abrahamic religions has a sacred text and engages it in spiritually enriching ways. For Judaism, that text is the Torah. Synagogues have a beautiful, handwritten scroll of this sacred text as the primary spiritual symbol of their worship service. Most basically, this comprises the Five Books of Moses that Christians also read as the first five books of our Bible. Contrary to some Christians' view of these books as "law," Jews see them as "teaching" or "way." Torah is seen as sacred story of the long-term relationship between God and the Jewish people.

A vital spiritual practice for Jews is to explore the Torah for new discoveries for life in the present age. Argument is frequent and acceptable, even expected; it is argument for the sake of God. Out of arguments in previous ages, the Talmud has reported minority opinions about the meaning or significance of a text. Rabbi Kushner notes, "When Jews disagree or argue about the meaning of Torah, they are actually helping one another become better Jews."[10]

Jews think of Torah as a beautiful orchard, and this view of Torah as orchard gives them guidance as to how to receive all the wisdom Torah contains. The Hebrew word for orchard is *pardes,* and it serves as an acrostic for the Jewish interpretation (exegesis) of Scripture. Each consonant letter of the Hebrew word stands for an interpretive layer of the Torah:

• The letter *pey* is the first letter of the Hebrew word *peshat,* meaning "surface" or "straight," and refers to the simple superficial story one might see in a first quick reading.
• The letter *resh* is the first letter of *remez.* This word means "hint." As one reads a story in Torah, what else does it remind one of? What clues or hints are there about something else, something deeper?
• The letter *dalet* is the first letter of *derash* which means "seek" or "inquire." One story in Torah may lead to thinking about and reflecting on other Torah stories. Comparison and reflection on the interplay between the stories can teach one about one's life.
• The letter *samech* is the first letter of *sod.* This word means "secret," not in the sense of something to withhold but rather something mysterious.

Thus, Torah is seen as an orchard with four possible avenues into discovery (the simple, the hint, the inquiring, and the secret). It provides many surprises and tells everything one needs to know. Jews see Proverbs 3:18 as describing Torah in this way: "It is a tree of life to those who hold on to it."[11]

For Muslims, the sacred text is the Qur'an. In 609 of the Common Era, Muhammad, then forty years old, was meditating in a cave near Mecca. He was frightened and startled to hear a voice saying "Recite!" Muslims believe that Muhammad, whom they regard as Prophet, received a direct message from God through the angel Gabriel. Frightened and overwhelmed, at first he only told his wife Kadijah, who believed he had received a divine revelation. In time, he told a small band of followers as well. The word Qur'an means "recite."

Muhammad received these "recitations," which were remembered and transcribed by his followers over the next twenty-one years until his death in 632. There are 114 of these recitations that make up the *suras* (chapters) of the Qur'an.

Qur'an is seen as a miracle. Much of it (particularly in its original Arabic) is gorgeous, soaring poetry, which Muslims believe could not have come from Muhammad himself, for he was an illiterate, unlettered man. For Muslims, the Qur'an is the ultimate guide. It is studied and recited. In the fasting month of Ramadan, the whole Qur'an (which is about the length of the Christian New Testament) is recited. An especially devout Muslim who memorizes the whole Qur'an is known as a *hafiz*.

The sacred text of Christians is the Bible, which consists of both the Old and New Testaments (covenants). More than three centuries ago, John Robinson told the pilgrims departing for the New World, "I am verily persuaded the Lord hath more truth yet to break forth out of His Holy Word." We of the Christian faith have trusted and followed that promise. Christians engage in personal Bible study and attend worship where the Bible is read, interpreted, and proclaimed. We gather for small-group Bible studies, some of which use a method called "Lectio Divina," where a Bible passage is read aloud multiple times, interspersed by times of silence for us to listen for the word for each of us from that particular Scripture. Many small groups also study the Bible by reading and then discussing together, as well as praying for one another, their church, community, and world.

Much more could be said of the Christian faith, of course. We treasure our sacred text and thus have perspective on other religious folks who treasure theirs.

Common Spiritual Practices

Another aspect that religions in the Abrahamic tradition hold in common is that each offers guidance on spiritual practices that strengthen and sustain one's faith. To this end, Islam provides "Five Pillars," which are ritual devotional responsibilities to help the faithful remember God constantly. They include the following:

- The confession of faith (*shahadah*), "There is no God but God, and Muhammad is the messenger of God," to be recited daily.
- The five daily prayers (*salat*) offered at prescribed times, the first before dawn, preceded by ritual cleansings, to stay focused on what truly matters.
- Charitable giving (*zakat*), 2½ percent of one's wealth is to be given annually to those in need.
- Fasting from sunrise to sundown during the lunar month of Ramadan (*sawm*), a reminder that all comes from God and that spiritual growth can be enhanced by self-denial.
- If one can afford it, at least once in a lifetime a pilgrimage (*hajj*) to the holy city of Mecca, a life-changing experience that makes one vividly aware of equality before God.

Judaism guides Jews into a number of practices to enrich the spiritual life as well. I shall focus on two. One is the practice of Sabbath. The Sabbath—a time of rest, renewal, and gladness—was a Jewish gift to the world. Biblical commandments instruct that Sabbath be extended to foreigners, servants, slaves, and animals. All are to be included in the rest and joy of the Sabbath. For some time, I have taken at least one class of seminarians with me to a Friday evening Shabbat

(Sabbath) service at a local synagogue. The form of services varied, but the central theme was always clear. From the parking lot on in, the greeting "Shabbat Shalom" would ring out, in word and song, time and again.

The other central spiritual practice of Judaism is prayer. One need only turn to the Book of Psalms, a large collection of prayer poems, to begin to tap the riches of prayer in the Jewish faith, a richness claimed by Christians as well. Rabbi Kushner says of the Book of Psalms, "Its words, like the words of other prayers in the traditional Jewish prayer book, are a script or musical score for words and songs that already exist within each of us and within all creation."[12] Kushner continues with this profound view of prayer:

> Sometimes the prayers seem to come from our own heart; at other times we find them written in the prayer book; at still other times they seem to be whispered by the wind. But, no matter where we find them, the words of prayers are already present. They need someone to speak them. By giving them a voice, we come closer to God.[13]

Since I am quoting a Jewish rabbi as I explore the Christian spiritual enrichment of prayer, we find how kindred are our views and practices of prayer, and how much we can receive from one another.

Traditions of a Deeper Mysticism

So far, we have been describing spiritual practices that are part of the larger body of each of these three major faith traditions. Each religion also has mystical traditions that some explore in depth. I will tell you just a bit about some of these. These little introductions are far too brief and incomplete. Though I cannot explore these traditions in any detail in this book, I want to acknowledge their existence.

For Muslims, mysticism takes the expression of Sufism, which began within a century of the founding of Islam. Its practitioners have seen it as expressing the true essence of Islam. Kabir Edmund Helminski writes that "Sufism is a way of life in which a deeper identity is discovered and lived. . . . Sufism is less a doctrine or a belief system than an experience and way of life."[14] Sufism is a means to activate our essential human qualities, Helminski says, and stands as a call to escape the present cultural tyranny, the tyranny of the ego. Rather, he suggests, Sufism is "the attribute of those who love."[15]

Over its more than twelve-hundred-year existence, Sufism has taken a variety of forms and practices, with the goal of opening the heart to experiences of the divine. Some scholars have used the metaphors of "drunk" and "sober" to characterize two basic forms of Sufism. The medium for the sober Sufi is prose and reason, with an emphasis on awe for God's power and thus strict adherence to Qur'anic (shariah) law, while the medium for the drunk or ecstatic Sufi is poetry and emotion, with an emphasis on the mercy and beauty of God, who can be approached more with love and ecstasy than awe and fear. The thirteenth-century Sufi mystic, theologian, and poet Rumi, as well as the twelfth-century "Whirling Dervishes" (who embraced an austere life of poverty but were known for their ecstatic frenzies), have been expressions of this aspect. They seek a "second knowing" that springs from a direct, personal experience of God.[16]

Author and professor Stephen Prothero tells of visiting with a shopkeeper in Jerusalem, a lifelong Sufi who said that real Islam is not about law but about experience. "It is about a heart-and-soul connection between the individual believer and God—the sort of crazy love that sets your whole being into dance. It needs no rituals, no rules . . . [which] only take us away from what is Really Real."[17]

For Judaism, the mystical practice is known as Kabbalah, which means "tradition." In recent years, a contemporary expression of some form of Kabbalah became a fascination, attracting a number of famous actors and singers. However, the tradition is much older and deeper than the recent fad. The foundational work for Kabbalah was articulated in the medieval books known as *The Zohar* (which means "splendor" or "radiance"). *The Zohar* first appeared in Spain in the thirteenth century CE and was published by a Jewish writer named

Moses de León. De León ascribed the work to Shimon bar Yochai ("Rashbi"), a rabbi of the second century during the Roman persecution.[18] It includes commentary on the mystical aspects of the Torah as well as material on mysticism, cosmogony, and psychology. It also contains discussions of the nature of God, the origin and structure of the universe, the nature of souls, and much more. As Rabbi Immanuel Schochet noted, the heart of Kabbalah and its teachings is not a compound of personal insights but is rather "an integral part of the Torah." There are reports of mystical experiences, visions, and more, but these are the effects of Kabbalah, not its essence.

I must admit that, although I honor this mystical tradition within Judaism, I have had a hard time intuiting into it. The biggest help to me in this regard is the novel *Kabbalah: A Love Story*,[19] written by the same Rabbi Lawrence Kushner whom I have often quoted in this chapter. Kushner weaves a story that spans thirteenth-century Spain, as well as several places-times in the twentieth and twenty-first centuries, and tells the story of three very different persons with closed hearts caught up in something mystical, unlocked by encounters with the *Zohar*. If this stirs your curiosity, I recommend you read the novel.

Christians as well have a long heritage of mystical teachings and practices that dates back to the first centuries of the early church. Throughout history, many Christians have longed for a closer relationship to God as known in Jesus Christ. A Christian mystic is a person drawn to Jesus—his life, teaching, death, and resurrection—and who is willing to invest in a deep spiritual search and intimate relationship with God. Ursula King, a scholar of spirituality, has written:

> The story of the Christian mystics is one of an all-consuming, passionate love affair between human beings and God. It speaks of the yearning, a burning desire for the contemplation and presence of the divine. . . . This yearning is a candle by the fire of divine love itself, which moves the mystics in their search and leads [them], often on arduous journeys, to discover and proclaim the all-encompassing love of God for humankind.[20]

Generally speaking, those pursuing Christian mysticism have been led one of two ways. One way is to solitude, withdrawing from society and ordinary life, originally into the desert or wilderness. The other has been to form communities where a group will meet several times a day for worship, reading-singing Scripture, and a life of prayer and service together.

In this latter regard, I was touched to read the award-winning author and poet Kathleen Norris's account of how she—a married, middle-aged Protestant—experienced the appeal of a Benedictine community. Norris wrote:

> I was a rank beginner, not sure what an abbey was. And I recall dragging both chatter and a bulging briefcase into . . . worship of the hours with me, not knowing what [it] was all about. But I also liked what I found there, and drank so deeply of monastic hospitality that when I went back home, I began dreaming about the place. My unconscious mind knew, long before I did, that I had received an invitation. I stood before an open door, and was being welcomed inside.[21]

She went on to rich experiences of learning and growing in the hospitality of the Benedictine monastic community, a source of spiritual growth in her Christian faith of which she was previously unaware.

All three Abrahamic religions have not only a way of spiritual growth for all drawn to that faith; each also has a tradition and path for those seeking a deeper, closer walk with God. However, the place where we of different religions relate to each other spiritually may be closer than that—much closer.

Spiritual Persons of Integrity, Ethics, Hospitality, and Compassion

Perhaps we are most closely drawn to one another across faith traditions when we hear about or meet and get to know persons formed by one of these religions, persons whose spirituality is seen in their kindness and compassion. These may be persons whose stories we read in books or in headlines—Malala Yousafzai, Ann Frank, and Mother Teresa, for example. Or they may be the people we encounter in our neighborhoods and communities.

I could speak of many such individuals in different religions, but I will speak of just one. Shakil is one of those persons for me. When I sought other people to serve on a committee to plan a Baptist-Muslim dialogue day, a mutual friend suggested Shakil, and upon invitation, he agreed to serve. As the committee progressed, he was a faithful and helpful member. We often met over the evening meal hour, and he would quietly excuse himself for washing and praying the Maghrib sundown prayer. He recruited friends, found a very reasonable caterer for our event, and hosted a table with generous gifts of information for all who wanted it. When we had our post-event committee meeting, Shakil came with gifts for each of us—a pen and pencil set on which he had engraved our names. A spiritual gift that came to me in the responsibility of planning that event was to meet and get to know Shakil.

Reflect, Discuss, Do

1. What are the spiritual ways—practices, experiences, persons, community—that are most enriching to you personally?

2. Whom from other denominations or religions do you admire for their spirituality and character?

3. This chapter speaks of five channels of shared spirituality: reverence for nature; love of our Holy Scriptures; spiritual practices; mystical traditions; and saintly people. Which of these have been means for you to experience another religion's spirituality? Tell someone about it.

4. **Do:** Learn more about the spiritual journey of someone you admire.

Notes

1. Stephen Prothero, *God Is Not One: The Eight Rival Religions That Run the World—and Why Their Differences Matter* (New York: HarperOne, 2010), 1.

2. Matthew Fox, *One River, Many Wells: Wisdom Springing from Global Faiths* (New York: Jeremy P. Tarcher/Penguin, 2004), 2.

3. Ibid., unnumbered dedication page.

4. Lawrence Kushner, *Jewish Spirituality: A Brief Introduction for Christians* (Woodstock, VT: Jewish Lights Publishing, 2001, 2002), 9.

5. Ibid., 10, 99.

6. Hamza Andreas Tzortzis, "What is Islamic Spirituality?" undated, accessed August 10, 2016, http://www.hamzatzortzis.com/1653/what-is-islamic-spirituality/.

7. Frederick M. Denny, "Islam and Ecology: A Bestowed Trust Inviting Balanced Stewardship," Yale University, The Forum on Religion and Ecology at Yale, undated, accessed August 1, 2016, http://fore.yale.edu/religion/islam.

8. Kushner, *Jewish Spirituality*, 28.

9. Ibid., 21.

10. Ibid., 45.

11. Ibid., 49–51.

12. Ibid., 81.

13. Ibid., 81–82.

14, Kabir Edmund Helminski, excerpt from *A Living Presence: A Sufi Way to Mindfulness and the Essential Self* (Threshold Books/Jeremy Tarcher, 1992), The Threshold Society, 2016, accessed August 23, 2016, http://sufism.org/lineage/sufism.

15. Ibid.

16. Prothero, *God Is Not One*, 59–60.

17. Ibid., 57.

18. "Zohar," Wikipedia, updated October 28, 2016, accessed August 14, 2016, https://en.wikipedia.org/wiki/Zohar.

19. Lawrence Kushner, *Kabbalah: A Love Story* (New York: Morgan Way Books, 2006).

20. Ursula King, "Christian Mystics Explained," 1999–2014, accessed August 28, 2016, http://www.christianmystics.com/basics/whatis.html.

21. Kathleen Norris, *Amazing Grace: A Vocabulary of Faith* (New York: Riverhead Books, 1998), 264.

CHAPTER THREE

God Is One; God Is Not One

Do not stop him; for whoever is not against you is for you.
—Luke 9:50

Indeed, I God have revealed to you Muhammad as I have revealed to Noah and to Abraham, Ishmael, Isaac, and the descendants of Israel. —Qur'an, 4:163

A basic step in being faithful in a multifaith world is to explore this question: Do various religions believe in and worship one and the same God or many gods? We continue to discuss the Abrahamic religions (Christianity, Judaism, and Islam).

Is God One? A Beginning — A Simple Answer with Complications

In Islam the first of the Five Pillars of faith is the affirmation: "There is no God but Allah, and Muhammad is the messenger of God."

It is important to understand who Allah is and how Allah is described and interpreted. At first look, the answer to this is rather simple. *Allah* is simply the word for "God" in Arabic. Charles Kimball, who for years worked among Christians in the Middle East, relates that Allah is the term Christians who speak Arabic use in worship when they pray and praise the God of Abraham and Sarah, of Jesus, and of the early church.[1] Indeed, Miroslav Volf tells of a ceremony of the Coptic Church (a Christian group dating back to the first century) in strongly Islamic Egypt. During that ceremony, a cross is tattooed

27

on a baby's wrist to identify the child as a Christian. When the tattoo is complete, the whole assembled congregation shouts "Allah!"[2] Therefore, we can use the Arabic term *Allah* to indicate that we all believe in one Divine Being, while we may have various understandings of that being.

However, it is not quite that simple. In the Muslim world, some Muslims reserve this Arabic word for God for themselves. For example, in 2007 the Malaysian Home Ministry started enforcing a 1986 law that prohibited the use of the word *Allah* in non-Muslim publications.[3] This ruling has been contested, but it is still true that some, perhaps only a few, would reserve this name for God to Islam alone.

Others in the Christian community also have reservations about this term. In late 2015 and into 2016, news media were giving attention to a controversy over this very topic at Wheaton College. One of its professors, Larycia Hawkins, a tenured political science professor, wore the *hijab* (traditional headscarf for Muslim women) through Advent in solidarity with Muslim sisters and brothers who were being harassed after terrorist attacks in Europe. She also posted on Facebook: "I stand in religious solidarity with Muslims because they, like me, a Christian, are people of the book. And as Pope Francis stated last week, we worship the same God."

Wheaton College requires faculty members to sign a statement of Christian faith. Hawkins had done so and believed that what she posted in no way violated that statement of faith. Officials at the college disagreed. "While Islam and Christianity are both monotheistic, we believe there are fundamental differences between the two faiths, including what they teach about God's revelation to humanity, the nature of God, the path to salvation and the life of prayer," Wheaton College said in a statement, as they initiated procedures to put Hawkins on academic probation and perhaps revoke her tenure.[4] Eventually, Wheaton College and Hawkins issued a joint statement that they had agreed to part ways, and she went to a position at the University of Virginia.

A Variety of Interpretations

The controversy sparked numerous blogs and essays addressing this question: Do Christians and Muslims worship the same God? Benjamin Corey—a missiologist, author, and speaker—wrote a blog that reminds us that Christianity, Judaism, and Islam all look to Abraham and his obedience to God as the founding source of their religious practice. In other words, Abraham founded a religion that, as Corey wrote, "went into three different streams." Corey noted that "Christianity, Islam and Judaism are attempting to worship and describe the same God (Abraham's God). . . . [This] doesn't mean . . . all religions are the same, equally valid, correct, or anything else." It simply means that all of us are trying to name the same divine entity.[5]

Corey's basic argument is that God/Allah is one, but that those who try to know God and reflect on the nature and attributes of God, each knowing and experiencing in part, might have quite different concepts of this one God. This point of view is upheld by many. We might mention the official view of the Roman Catholic Church. When, as Hawkins noted, Pope Francis stated that "we worship the same God," he was echoing the important document issued by the second Vatican Council in 1965, the "Nostra Aetate." Here, in part, is what it says:

> The Church has also a high regard for the Muslims. They worship God, who is one, living and subsistent, merciful and almighty, the Creator of heaven and earth . . . who has spoken to [humankind]. They strive to submit themselves without reserve to the hidden decrees of God, just as Abraham submitted himself to God's plan, to whose faith Muslims eagerly link their own. Although not acknowledging him as God, they venerate Jesus as a prophet, his Virgin Mother they also honor, and even at times devoutly invoke. Further, they await the day of judgment and the reward of God following the resurrection of the dead. For this reason they highly esteem an upright life and worship God, especially by way of prayer, alms-deeds and fasting.[6]

To this I add the witness of a learned Muslim, Imam Yahya Hendi, when he spoke to the College of St. Elizabeth in Morristown, New Jersey: "Islam is not believed by Muslims to be a new religion; rather, it is the same religion Abraham and other prophets and early scriptures called their followers to."[7] This statement is frequently repeated to me when I visit an Islamic Center. Islam is not a new religion, but is part of a line going back to the one God who spoke to Abraham.

There is widespread, but by no means unanimous, consensus that these three Abrahamic faiths address and speak of the same God, whatever the language, and that we concur on a number of things we believe about God even as we differ on others. (The same might be said about the understanding of God from denomination to denomination or Christian to Christian.)

Where Believers in One God May Agree or Differ

Can we name the ways these religions concur? Islamic scholar John L. Esposito, at the outset of a course on world religions, offers his view of this agreement: "All three faiths share a profound monotheism, belief in the one, transcendent God, who is creator, sustainer, and ruler of the universe." Furthermore, "all believe in angels, Satan, prophets, revelation, moral accountability and responsibility, divine judgment, and eternal reward or punishment."[8]

At first, Esposito's list of shared beliefs sounds reassuring. However, when I read it a second and third time, I realized that there are in fact wide variations among Christians, not to mention the other religions, in what we believe about some of those items of presumed shared belief. Christians, Muslims, and Jews may disagree as to what belief in the "one transcendent God" means. Stephen Prothero speaks of "hard" monotheism and "soft" monotheism.[9] Soft monotheism is Christian belief in the Trinity, by which we affirm that one God exists in three Persons, including the God-incarnate, Jesus. Hard monotheism is belief in one God with no divisions, distinctions, or "persons" within this one God. (We will revisit belief about Jesus in chapter nine.)

Religious art reflects these variations. For Muslims and Jews, God should not be represented in art; both Jewish and Muslim art emphasizes calligraphy. Traditional Christian art depicts many views of Jesus and the Holy Family. That is a fairly minor difference. But the concept of the Triune God of Christianity—typically interpreted by others as multiple gods—has been and may be a stumbling block to effective mutual dialogue.

I believe and hope that Christian-Jewish-Muslim dialogue can make progress on the conversation about the Trinity. That may be naïve in light of all who have debated this topic over the ages. Still, Christians might suggest that "God in three persons" speaks of God in three personas, or roles, or aspects of relationship of the one God with us. Former archbishop of Canterbury Rowan Williams put it into sophisticated theological language. He wrote in response to an invitation of dialogue about the two great commandments: "God exists in a threefold pattern of interdependent action . . . there is only one divine nature and reality."[10] I would hope that these suggested descriptions of Trinity might meet a positive response. In my opinion, there is a connection between what I summarized about Trinity and the Muslims' many names-descriptors for Allah. All but one of the *suras* (chapters) in the Qur'an begins with the phrase about Allah: "All Compassionate and All Merciful." Elsewhere in the Qur'an, Allah is called "Sovereign Lord," "the Holy One," "Peace," "the Keeper of Faith," "the Guardian," "the Majestic," "the Compeller," and "the Superb." It is said that Muhammad spoke of Allah having ninety-nine names. Some Muslim leaders divide these many names into feminine names of beauty and masculine names of majesty. But Allah is beyond gender.[11]

As Miroslav Volf has noted, this issue must be treated carefully and respectfully, for the oneness of God (*tawhid*) is at the very heart of Islam and a central issue for conversations with Christians about the nature of God.[12] Further, in Judaism, the *Shema* proclaims, "Hear O Israel, the Lord thy God is one."

While we may be able to work our way into understanding one another on such difficult topics as the Trinity, the Abrahamic faiths will need to agree to disagree on the Incarnation. We Christians believe with the apostle Paul that "in Christ, God was reconciling the world to himself" (2 Corinthians 5:19). This in turn influences what we find essential to believe. Muslims and Jews do not believe that God would enter into a human body and human existence in such a way. Muslims see Jesus in a quite different role, as an honored prophet. They see Muhammad as an honored prophet as well, although Muhammad is the last of the prophets. And Jews disagree with Paul that Jesus was "the Christ"—which is the Greek translation of "messiah," meaning "anointed one." They believe the promised messiah has not yet come.

We have walked around views of Allah-God-Yahweh from same, to utterly different, to similar or related, to nuanced with many points of contact and also points of difference. If this discussion has made sense, a joint wisdom can emerge for our interfaith conversations. It is this: We have a similar starting place, but we need to be sensitive about presumptions of sameness and instead ask many questions related to beliefs about God's nature and what we mean when we affirm God as one.

A Comparative Religion View of Our Differences

Perhaps these interfaith conversations about whom we worship may be even more complex than I have described so far. I have been exploring how to understand and talk about our belief in the Divine One. Now I turn our attention to another important scholar of religion, who looks at how religions have developed and what impact they have had. His is a "comparative religion" approach (more about that later in this chapter).

In his book *God Is Not One: The Eight Rival Religions That Run the World—and Why Their Differences Matter*, Stephen Prothero contends that those who write about the oneness of all religions "are not describing the world, but reimagining it. They are hoping that their hope will call up in us feelings of brotherhood and sisterhood."[13]

He isn't wrong. That *is* what I am hoping as I write this book. I desire a deeper understanding and community between persons of different religions. So it is important for me to listen to Prothero (and tell you a little about his view) so that we understand with more depth how complex is the journey we're attempting.

He points out that while world religions may converge on matters such as ethics, they differ deeply on doctrine, ritual, mythology, experience, law, and much more. Adherents of religion find these matters deeply important, and indeed, are often life-determining, with real effects in people's lives. Rituals are important to religious practitioners, such as the rites of baptism and Eucharist for Christians, the Hajj to Mecca for Muslims, and the Passover for Jews. Religions may determine that one may not marry a Christian or Jew or Hindu or Muslim. People have fought and killed over religious differences for centuries. Religion also matters economically, politically, and militarily. Therefore, Prothero suggests, "What we need on this furiously religious planet is a realistic view of where religious rivals clash and where they can cooperate."[14]

He begins his analysis by suggesting that what the world's religions share is a starting point, and what we share most fundamentally is the conviction that something is wrong with the world. Life is out of balance; something has gone awry. Religions differ, however, in diagnosing what has gone wrong, and, therefore, what the prescribed solution is. Although the world's religions are related, says Prothero, they are more like "second cousins than identical twins."[15]

Prothero offers a four-part approach to understanding the essence of what each religion articulates:

- a *problem*;
- a *solution* to this problem, which also serves as the religious goal;
- a *technique* (or techniques) for moving this problem to its solution; and
- an *exemplar* (or exemplars) who chart the path from problem to solution.[16]

To demonstrate this, he offers the example that in Christianity, the problem is sin, and the solution or goal is salvation. The means for achieving this is some combination of faith and good works, and the exemplars may be the disciples of Scripture, the saints of old (especially for the Roman and Eastern churches), and ordinary people of faith (for most Protestants).

(By contrast, in Buddhism, the problem is suffering, and the solution or goal is nirvana. The technique for achieving this is the Noble Eightfold Path that includes such classic practices as meditation and chanting. Various branches of Buddhism each have their exemplars.)

Prothero suggests that in Islam "the problem is self-sufficiency, the hubris of acting as if you can get along without God, who alone is self-sufficient."[17] The solution, then, is the way of submission.

In speaking of Judaism, he offers the contrast that if Christianity is about doctrine (as regards sin and salvation) and Islam about ritual, then Judaism is about narrative. Its Scriptures contain stories of wrongdoing, punishment, exile, and return. Similarly, the Hebrew Scriptures tell stories of covenant, breach, and new covenant.[18] Prothero concludes that in Judaism then, the problem is disobedience and alienation; the solution is repentance, exile, and return. This is reinforced through ritual practices, including festivals, that help keep alive their memory in story.

In contrast to those who believe that God/Allah is one, Prothero sees the three religions as having three different Gods/gods—or perhaps three different roles for God in response to each religion's perceived deepest need, whether salvation, submission, or return. In Prothero's view, each religion has emerged over the centuries and developed institutions, rituals, requirements for religious leaders, obligatory practices, and forbidden practices. These have arisen from initial convictions about what one needs from God and how one secures the most needed gift from God.

I won't discuss here the way Prothero describes the other five religions he explores. However, we will note his wise counsel that one of the temptations of any religion "is to mistake [itself] for the Ultimate To Which It Points."[19] For example, a Christian's temptation might be to worship Christianity—our traditions, our institutions, our sanctuaries, our doctrines—rather than the God in Christ who is our Source. Other religions face a similar temptation.

As I mentioned earlier, Prothero points out two ways to talk about religion, and he is engaging the second way. One is the way we know best, the way of religion practiced as we have been taught, with attendance at worship services, memorizing of Scripture, practicing our rituals, following the ethics of our faith, doing it all from within the faith heritage we have inherited or chosen. The second way is the secular way to speak of religion, often called comparative religion. This way "does not assume that religion in general, or any religion in particular, is either true or false, because to make such an assumption is to be talking about religion religiously. It aims instead simply to observe and report, as objectively as possible, on this thing human beings do for good or for ill (or both)."[20] While Prothero describes each religion appreciatively and sympathetically, I have been summarizing his secular view on religions.

I find this method helpful, but only to a point. While his descriptions help me gain a perspective on the difficulties and barriers among persons of different religions, I want to find a way around those problems, both the broad perspective and the in-depth encounter. How can people of faith and goodwill transcend the barriers so that they meet, listen, and come to understand one another, and can commit to shared peacemaking?

One Believer's Voyage of Discovery and Insight

As I consider these questions, I have been helped by my friend Rev. Lee Rader's reflection on her story. Lee recalls an experience that was important for her, as out of her conservative Christian past, she struggled with the concept of pluralism. The following passages quote Lee's words liberally with her permission.[21]

During her clinical pastoral education, Lee made a hospital call on a Hindu man and his wife. The man was suffering badly with leg pain. His wife sat close by, brow heavy with worry, "her forehead bearing the distinctive red dot or *tilaka*." Feeling led to pray for the man, Lee asked him what he did to express hope in his tradition.

"We pray," he answered.

"Then may I pray with you?" Lee asked.

For a short time, the man and his wife had a lively conversation in Hindi, and then he said yes. So Lee offered a brief prayer for the man, his circumstance, his pain. At the end of the prayer, the man exclaimed with great excitement, "Your God and my God the same!"

Lee recalls, "I sheepishly agreed and then left the room feeling at once gladness and a trace of heresy." Later, she related the story and her questions to her peer group of ministers in training. Her supervisor helped in her reflection. He asked her what she knew about women in India. She responded that they are probably not regarded on an equal basis with men. He then asked what she thought the man and his wife were discussing in Hindi. "They were probably deciding if they should allow me to pray," she said. The supervisor continued to probe, "Probably so. So if this Hindu man was willing to be inclusive of you, a woman, in his realm, can you find it in your heart to be inclusive of him in your realm?"

Lee found this experience and reflection revealing, as to "how it challenged my exclusive theological framework"—the assumption and conviction that only Christians knew and prayed to the true God. But then will she lose any framework whatsoever? Where does one find balance in this world of pluralism?

A few years later, Lee found an image and perspective that, in her words, "helped me steady the swinging pendulum" of close-mindedness and undisciplined openness. She was part of a three-person crew in an international sailboat race across the Pacific from Los Angeles to Osaka, Japan. During her long watches, she had much time to reflect. She recalls,

> The sails helped me with my search. There were times when a "broad reach" was called for. The sails were let out as far as possible, almost perpendicular to the boat and we "ran" with the wind. . . . I likened the broad reach to the breadth and the depth of the rich and various ways

spirituality expresses herself in humankind across this glorious wide earth.

But there were also times when a "close haul" was called for. In this instance, we were sailing very close to the wind. The wind was blowing nearly across our bow and in order to make any headway the sails had to be hauled in almost parallel to the length of the boat. I likened the close haul to the "narrow" distinctiveness of Christianity and of any other of the major world religions.

Now the truth of the matter was that if we became too "narrow" and sailed directly into the wind, we landed ourselves in "irons" and lost all wind completely. On the other extreme, if we "ran" with the wind, we risked an uncontrolled jibe when the stern passes through the wind and the boom whips from one side of the boat to the other. This can be quite dangerous. In this instance, in a sense we let ourselves be too free with no distinctiveness at all.

The sails taught me that both extremes—the broad reach and the close haul (and all the points of sail in between)— are needed in order to catch the wind, or spirit if you will. The model of the sails helped me claim the distinctiveness of my own Christian tradition and its fathomless depth, while also marveling in the endless places and peoples in which the great Spirit of us all resides.

Jesus of the Gospels moved among those of different races and religions in his world with openness to encounter, responsiveness to their needs, and candor. As we walk the road of a multifaith world, I hope we follow this example, also guided by the message Lee heard in the sails on her ocean voyage.

Reflect, Discuss, Do

1. What were your thoughts on whether various religions believe in the same God before you read this chapter?

2. Which of the perspectives offered in this chapter make sense to you as you sort out this question?

3. To what extent can we dialogue with persons of other religions if we answer "no, we do not worship the same God"? If so, how? What are the reasons for your answer?

4. What do you take away from Lee's story of her encounter with the Hindu man and her reflections on her ocean voyage?

5. **Do:** Interview someone whose beliefs about God differ from yours. Ask what the person believes about God and why. If the person asks you the same thing, answer as best you can.

Notes

1. Charles Kimball, *Striving Together: A Way Forward in Christian-Muslim Relations* (Maryknoll, NY: Orbis Books, 1991), 19.

2. Miroslav Volf, *Allah: A Christian Response* (New York: HarperOne, 2011), 82.

3. Ibid., 80.

4. Manya Brachear Pashman, "Wheaton College, professor at impasse after her suspension," *Chicago Tribune,* December 24, 2015, accessed July 15, 2016, http://www.chicagotribune.com/news/local /breaking/ct-wheaton-college-hijab-larycia-hawkins-1223-met-20151222-story.html.

5. Benjamin L. Corey, "Yes, Christians and Muslims Worship the Same God (But Here's What That Means & Doesn't)," Patheos: Hosting the Conversation on Faith, Dec. 17, 2015, accessed July 5, 2016, http://www.patheos.com/blogs/formerlyfundie/yes-christians-and-mus lims-worship-the-same-god-but-heres-what-that-means-doesnt/.

6. United States Conference of Catholic Bishops. Second Vatican Council, Nostra Aetate 3, October 28, 1965, accessed July 20, 2016, http://www.usccb.org/beliefs-and-teachings/ecumenical-and-interreli gious/interreligious/islam/vatican-council-and-papal-statements-on-islam.cfm.

7. Imam Yahya Hendi, "The Story of Abraham: A journey of hope for all," [*sic* lowercase] College of St. Elizabeth, July 19, 2003, ac-

cessed November 21, 2017, http://imamyahyahendi.com/library_ar
ticles_2.htm.

8. John L. Esposito, *Great World Religions: Islam* (Chantilly, VA:
The Teaching Company Limited Partnership, 2003), 4.

9. Stephen Prothero, *God Is Not One: The Eight Rival Religions
That Run the World—and Why Their Differences Matter* (New York:
HarperOne, 2010), 36.

10. Rowan Williams, quoted in Volf, *Allah*, 128.

11. Prothero, *God Is Not One*, 36

12. Volf, *Allah*, 129.

13. Prothero, *God Is Not One*, 6–7.

14. Ibid., 4.

15. Ibid., 13.

16. Ibid., 14.

17. Ibid., 32.

18. Ibid., 243–44.

19. Ibid., 62.

20. Ibid., 336.

21. Lee L. Rader, "Fresh Winds in an Understanding of Pluralism,"
The Journal of Pastoral Care 51, no.1 (Spring 1997), 115–116.

CHAPTER FOUR

Conversation or Conversion?

Be ready at any time to give a quiet and reverent answer to any [one] who wants a reason for the hope that is within you. — 1 Peter 3:15b, Phillips

Call to the way of your Lord with wisdom and fair preaching, and argue with them in the best manner possible.
—Qur'an 16:125

When I attended a session on Christian-Muslim relations at a recent national gathering of my denomination, it soon became clear that not all of us had the same reason for being there. Some of us wanted to exchange information, beliefs, and experiences for the purpose of building mutually enriching relationships. Others of us spoke of forming connections with Muslims for the hope of convincing them to believe in Jesus as Savior and Lord and to become part of the Christian faith community. The differences in purpose among us felt sharp and clear.

Conversion, Conversation, or a Combination?

When we engage in interreligious contacts, is our purpose conversation, or is it conversion? Or both? Or both with one the priority, and the other a possibility? And if our intent is conversion, what might be ethical and respectful ways to go about it? What are the unethical or disrespectful methods and styles to avoid?

(I acknowledge that, for the sake of exploring this question, I will be misusing the term "conversion." The theological truth is that no human being converts another person. It is God who speaks to a heart and changes or converts it.)

Judaism — Not a Missionary Religion

One of the three religions we are discussing—Judaism—has a clear answer that is a distinct contrast to the other two. Simply put, the position of Judaism is this: we don't seek converts, and we don't want anyone attempting to convert us. Conversation for mutual enrichment and enlightenment is welcomed.

In his book *Jewish Spirituality: A Brief Introduction for Christians,* Rabbi Lawrence Kushner summarizes this position well:

> Judaism is not a world-conquering spiritual tradition. To be sure, we welcome converts and (most of us, anyway) think we have a pretty good thing. But our success as Jews is not indexed to the number of non-Jews we persuade to join us. Whether or not there are a lot of Jews or just a few is God's business; ours is trying to live according to God's way. For this reason, most Jews find the frequent missionary attempts to convert Jews unintelligible and insulting. . . . Judaism is . . . a complete, self-contained religion; it needs nothing . . . to complete it.[1]

Of course, it is important to note that Judaism is not a monolithic faith. It has four primary traditions and expressions: Orthodox (including the Hasidic sect), Reform, Conservative, and Reconstructionist. (A fifth expression would be the self-identified secular or non-religious Jew.) But in any of these forms, Judaism is *not* a missionary religion.

Christianity — An Historically Missionary Religion

Both Christianity and Islam are quite different from Judaism in this regard. Both began as tiny movements that grew swiftly and spread vastly. They are both "missionary religions."

Christianity began as Jesus drew a small number of followers, teaching and training them as his disciples. They scattered when he was arrested and killed, revived when they witnessed his Resurrection, and were empowered by God's Spirit on Pentecost. Given the commission to go into the world and make disciples of all the nations, they did just that. In the early centuries, missionary teams traveled throughout the Roman Empire, inviting faith in Jesus and establishing churches. In the fourth century, under Emperor Constantine, Christianity became the official cultural religion of his realm. In later centuries, Christianity also grew partly as an accompaniment to conquest, colonialism, and empire building.

While for centuries Roman Catholic missionaries had been found wherever European nations had established colonies, in the late eighteenth and following centuries, Protestants discovered their own missionary ardor. They sent wave upon wave of missionaries to most parts of the known earth, with ministries of healing, education, and preaching for conversion. In some places, this call to embrace Christianity had very small response; in other places, large populations embraced the new faith. Out of these various methods and efforts, Christianity (one of the youngest of the world religions) has grown from that small band of Jesus' followers to billions, an estimated one-third of all the humans on our planet.

We Christians are a varied lot today. Within Christianity we find those who are Roman Catholic, Eastern Orthodox (with different cultural branches, Greek and Russian being the largest), and a wide variety of Protestants (mainline, evangelical, charismatic, and emergent), as well as less orthodox traditions such as the Church of Jesus Christ of Latter-Day Saints (Mormons) and Jehovah's Witnesses. Expressions of Christianity are changing and perhaps weakening, particularly in America and Europe, while growing in many other parts of the world. Still, an important element in our collective faith memory is the story of witness and response, of growth and conversion, and the vitality this has afforded our collective Christianity.

Islam — Another Missionary Religion

Islam has a parallel history. From the small band of followers led by Muhammad, a vast multitude of followers have come. Islam has always proclaimed itself as both a religion and a way of life, for government and society as well as for individuals. Some of its early expansion was military-political, as the empires under its influence grew throughout the Middle East. In fact, in its seventh-century beginnings, through the combination of missionary zeal and military prowess, Islamic influence extended from India to Spain. Persons were not forced to become Muslim when their country came under Islamist rule, but if they did, they were expected to remain within that faith community. Sometimes those who refused conversion, instead retaining their own religious identity, might be afforded protective status in exchange for an extra taxation.

In the last century, Islam has become the fastest-growing religion in the world. Its percentage of the global population almost doubled, from 12 percent in 1900 to 22 percent in 2017. The World Religion Database estimates that presently Islam is growing 33 percent faster than Christianity. Part of this rapid growth is due to the high birth rates in a number of nations where Islam is the predominant religion: Indonesia, Pakistan, Bangladesh, India, Egypt, and Iran, for example.[2] However, a significant portion of the growth comes from conversions.

As with Christianity and Judaism, Islam is varied. Within Islam are two primary branches—Sunni and Shi'a—as well as a variety of schools within each sect, including practitioners of Sufi mysticism. There are also less orthodox groups that claim to be Muslim in America and elsewhere. Islam is found in a wide range of cultures and participates in a variety of governments. In North America, an Islamic Center or mosque is a place where Muslims from many nations and cultures gather to practice and encourage one another's faith.

Both Islam and Christianity face questions on how faith can change and prosper in a fast-changing culture, with its technology, social media, diversity, and varied cultural expectations. These two historic missionary religions, each with followings in the billions, come into more frequent contact with each other now than ever before. We who are a part of them wonder, what now? How do we relate to each other in this place and this time? Do we seek to convert each other, or do we attempt a conversation so that we understand each other—and ourselves—more deeply?

Conversion Stories

No matter how we answer the questions regarding our purpose in interfaith contacts, some individuals do choose to convert from one religion to another and to then write or tell about their experiences. Perhaps we can learn if we listen to a few of those stories.

Nabeel Qureshi — Muslim to Christian

In his book *Seeking Allah, Finding Jesus*, Nabeel Qureshi tells the story of his conversion.[3] He begins with his childhood and the joys of growing up in a devout Muslim family: the shared love, the deeply enriching spiritual practices, and the local and larger community of Muslim worship and social ties. In college he became a close friend to David, a forensics teammate and a devout and informed Christian. The two of them loved a good debate and enjoyed many discussions, arguments, and skirmishes about their religious beliefs. In the process Nabeel gradually began to lose confidence in some of the basics of his Islamic faith and disappointing information about Muhammad. Further, his resistance to Christian doctrinal teachings about the divinity of Christ, the Crucifixion, and the Resurrection gradually diminished. He found himself drawn to become a Christian but resisted. This was in part out of loyalty to his heritage and his parents' love for him, as well as his fear of what his conversion might do to his family life.

Then one night he had a dream that he was convinced was given to him by God, and he concluded he had no choice but to confess his faith in Christ. The impact on his family was as hard as he had feared. His decision devastated his parents. After recovering from the initial shock, his family made two things clear to him: they felt utterly betrayed, and they loved him regardless. They have remained in relationship with one another despite the challenges. Nabeel is now in Christian ministry and concludes, "All suffering is worth it to follow Jesus."[4]

Jerald F. Dirks — Christian to Muslim

Jerald Dirks grew up deeply involved in Methodist church life in rural Kansas. In his late teens, he felt drawn to ministry. He enrolled in Harvard University and, as an undergraduate, took a rigorous two-semester course in comparative religion, taught by a renowned scholar.[5]

Throughout his education at Harvard University and Harvard Divinity School, Jerald was given awards and scholarships, along with opportunities for ministry, including preaching. In these ministry opportunities, he was well received, but something did not feel right to him. He was struggling with the intellectual integrity of being a minister. His study of ancient biblical texts "raised serious and disturbing questions about such basic Christian doctrines as the trinity of God, the 'sonship' of Jesus Christ, the actual historicity of the crucifixion event and the 'atonement in the blood.'"[6] Shortly after he finished divinity school, he left parish ministry permanently.

For the next nineteen years, he was, in his words, an "atypical Christian." He writes, "I had a deep and profound belief in God and in the teachings of Jesus Christ, but I could find no satisfactory expression for those beliefs within the confines of contemporary Christianity."[7] Then he came into informal contact with the Muslim community. He and his wife had an avid interest in the history of Arabian horses and engaged Arabic speakers who were also Muslim to translate materials for them. This led to friendship with Jamal and being impressed with his devotion and quality of life.

In time, Jamal introduced Jerald and his wife to others in the local Islamic community. It was in Jamal and others that Jerald saw the reverence-filled life of compassion and integrity for which he had longed. This led him into a period of both intense study of Islam and, at the same time, an inner resistance to accepting and embracing it. He spent a long period of time contemplating what to do. Then, during a trip to the Middle East, someone asked him in Arabic if he was a Muslim. With his basic knowledge of Arabic, he answered, *Nam,* which means yes. Jerald reflects, "The ordained minister who was an 'atypical Christian' had become a Muslim despite all of his psychological resistances, intellectual rationalization and verbal gymnastics."[8]

Jewish Identity and Conversions — Both Ways

Shalom Goldman, professor of religion at Middlebury College, explores the changing landscape of Jewish identity by telling the stories of seven twentieth-century converts. We cannot tell all seven here but will take a look at three.

Madeleine Ferraille (1920–2000) was born French Catholic but suspected that she was, and longed to be, Jewish. She was attracted to ancient history, including Jewish history; she also ardently read and explored a Bible given to her by the Salvation Army. Her views were further shaped and disillusioned by the fall of France in World War II as well as by its complicity in the persecution of Jews. Searching for a religion with a high moral code, Madeleine found a Reform rabbi to instruct her in Judaism. Upon conversion, she took the new name of Ruth Ben David. Goldman notes that what was true of Ruth was true of the other converts whose stories he tells, which was "a feeling that only with conversion does one begin to feel at peace."[9] However, Goldman notes that for Ruth, "conversion to Judaism was not the end of a process, but the beginning of one."[10] Indeed, it was the beginning of a lifelong spiritual search. In time she moved from Reform Judaism to Orthodox and eventually to what she considered the most authentic Jewish community, the ultra-Orthodox Haredi Jews.[11]

Goldman also tells the story of another convert from the same time and location. *Aaron Lustiger (1926–2007)* was the child of nonreligious Polish Jewish parents who had migrated to France. With the German invasion of France in 1940, he was acutely aware of the peril his family faced as Jews, though non-adherent. This led him on a spiritual search for answers. Like Madeleine, Aaron discovered a Protestant Bible and started reading it. His reading of the New Testament convinced him that Christianity was the fulfillment of Judaism. When asked if this marked his conversion, he responded, "It was more like a crystallization than a conversion."[12] At age fourteen, he sought baptism as a Roman Catholic. He saw this step as the fulfillment of his Judaism, but his decision scandalized his parents.

Now known as Jean-Marie Lustiger, he studied at a Catholic lycée (for his secondary education). According to Goldman, with a "beginner's mind" he was entranced by "a Christian life of rigor and beauty."[13] He attended Mass daily and found himself drawn to the priesthood, where he could engage the acts of religious devotion even more intensely. As part of his studies for the priesthood, he led a group on what was his first visit to the Holy Land. The beauty of the land, as well as the opportunity to visit and pray at the sites where Christians believe Jesus died and was buried, was a "pivotal moment in his spiritual development . . . a type of 'fifth gospel.'"[14]

Lustiger was ordained a Roman Catholic priest in 1954 and served as chaplain at the Sorbonne in France for five years. In 1959 he became director of Richleiu Center, which trains university chaplains and counsels students. He became vicar of the Parish of Sainte-Jeanne-de-Chantal in Paris, then bishop of Orleans, and shortly after that, the archbishop of Paris. As a Catholic leader with Jewish roots, he was often asked to adjudicate conflicts and crises in Christian-Jewish relations. For the most part, the European Jewish community saw him as a trusted negotiating partner. They, however, rejected his claim that he was still a faithful practicing Jew.[15]

Throughout the rest of his life, Lustiger participated in numerous activities to sensitize Christians to Jewish concerns and represent Christians in both negotiations and commemorative events among Jews. When he died, the controversy regarding whether he was a Jew or a Christian continued. He requested that a relative recite Kaddish, a traditional Jewish prayer, at his funeral. He was remembered as a "friend of the Jews" or perhaps "a good-bad Jew."[16]

Another story of conversion concerns a poor, illiterate farmer named *Donato Manduzio (1885–1948)*, who was born Roman Catholic in San Nicandro in southeast Italy. Drafted into the army, he suffered an injury to his legs and spent the rest of his life unable to walk. However, while hospitalized he learned to read and became an ardent reader of whatever was available. Upon his return his home, he became known as a faith healer still in good standing as a Catholic, a gifted storyteller, and an able community organizer. He also had prophetic visions from time to time. He developed a circle of friends-followers that numbered about fifty.

At about the same time as his first prophetic vision, he was given a Bible and read it avidly. He focused on the Hebrew Bible (Old Testament); its prohibitions against magic and divination impressed him, and so he abandoned these practices. Further, he was drawn to its teaching about the conduct of life and the observances of the Sabbath.

Donato's followers gathered weekly to study the biblical narratives and his discourses on them. He recorded in his journal, "Immediately, I proclaimed to the people the one God and the words of Sinai and how the Creator rested on the seventh day."[17] Manduzio considered himself a prophet like the biblical prophets. Guided by his reading of the Scriptures, he asked his followers to remove all crucifixes, rosaries, and other Christian artifacts from their homes because he saw them as a form of idolatry. Some resisted and turned away, while others followed. They believed that they had become Jews—and were the only Jews in the world. San Nicandro was an extremely remote village in southern Italy. They had no knowledge of other Jews and were amazed to learn eventually (perhaps from a traveling merchant) that not only were there Jews in the world but even in Italy.

Immediately Manduzio contacted Jewish leaders and requested instruction and confirmation as Jews. That request was in 1930. Response was slow and interrupted. World War II and its destructive imprint on the Jews intervened. But some sixteen years later, and not without conflicts (such as whether Manduzio could be a modern-day prophet), the first conversion ceremonies for these converts of

San Nicandro took place.[18] Donato Manduzio and his followers provide another story of conversion—persons who are converted to a whole new way of life, reading the Bible, and being guided by a local leader in isolation from (and ignorance of) the recognized leaders of that religion.

Goldman tells these stories to explore the question of the stretching and straining of the concept of Jewish identity. Traditionally, one was a Jew, either through the bloodline of one's mother or through instruction by an orthodox rabbi. But, as he demonstrates, this definition has been challenged in various ways by people's lived experiences.

I hear similar stories when I talk with persons who have converted from one religion to another. What do we take from these stories? They seem to say that some feel the need to convert from a religion of their heritage to another. They may experience a hunger, a nudge, a restlessness. Some are not only open to conversion but eagerly seek it, indeed feel compelled toward it. When we hear these conversion stories, we need to be mindful that many, or perhaps most, people of faith are deeply rooted and enriched in their own faith heritage. For them, interfaith conversation needs a different purpose and conclusion other than conversion.

The Close Relationship of Conversation and Conversion

When I first noticed this conversation-conversion conflict, I thought a greater distance existed between those wanting conversation and those wanting conversion than I am now discovering. In any conversation of this sort, there will be mutual witness and enrichment. And any witness hoping for conversion must begin with respectful conversation.

In "Why Do Muslims Call Others to Islam?" author Aisha Stacey writes: "If you discovered something so amazing you felt like jumping up and down in excitement, what is the first thing you would want to do? . . . If you discover the meaning of life or the secrets of the universe, what would you do with that knowledge? If you worked out a way of banishing fear and sadness and replacing it with eternal happiness, what would you do?"[19] Stacey suggests that most would not be able to contain their excitement and would want to tell as many persons as possible. That is one reason Muslims want to witness. Another reason is that "it involves obeying the commands of God, following in the footsteps of the prophets, and gathering rewards in the hope of attaining eternal peace and happiness in the Afterlife."[20]

Similarly, the document "Christian Witness in a Multi-Religious World," prepared by a study team and endorsed by international bodies of Catholics, mainline Protestants, and Evangelicals, conveys a strong motivation to witness. In speaking of a basis for Christian witness, they write: "For Christians, it is a privilege and joy to give an accounting for the hope that is within them and to do so with gentleness and respect." Further, "Jesus Christ is the supreme witness. . . . Christian witness is always a sharing in his witness, which takes the form of proclamation of the kingdom, service to the neighbor, and the total gift of self even if that act of giving leads to the cross."[21]

Whether conversion is a possibility or a priority, what guidance is available for how to engage in this process of interfaith conversation and potential conversion?

The persons I have been quoting as advocates for a stronger emphasis on witness than conversion are aware of some of the problems and criticisms of earlier missionary and witness efforts. They have given careful thought to this question: How can one do this witness in a manner that is worthy of the One of whom they witness?

I would like to point to two of the many resources that address this question. One is the interdenominational team that crafted the document "Christian Witness in a Multi-Religious World" quoted above. The other is author, speaker, and missionary David Shenk. Both offer lists of twelve principles (or guidelines or paths). These principles are briefly described in twelve paragraphs in the interdenominational document, while Shenk discusses these twelve principles in the twelve chapters of his award-winning book *Christian. Muslim. Friend.: Twelve Paths to Real Relationship*.[22] Some distinctions and some similarities are found in these two lists. It is beyond my purpose to explore all twelve in detail for each, but I will highlight a few salient points.

Guidance in Witness—Missionary David W. Shenk

David Shenk is a widely respected man who has devoted his life to this topic. He is a missionary commissioned by the Mennonite Church (an historic peace denomination), and he has engaged in life-long ministry among Muslim people, first in Somalia, then Kenya, and then the United States. He currently works as a consultant on this topic globally. Shenk has invested fifty years in this calling, and his book on the paths to true interfaith relationships was selected as the 2016 *Christianity Today* Book of the Year in missions and the global church.

I was impressed by how Shenk balances these two aspects of dialogue/friendship and witness in his book and how he brought them together, time and again. "I write this book," he explains by way of introduction, "with the conviction that every Muslim should have a Christian friend and every Christian should have a Muslim friend."[23] That sounds like dialogue. Indeed, he has coauthored a book with a Muslim friend, Badru Kateregga, called *A Christian and a Muslim in Dialogue*.[24] Their book contains authentic and respectful dialogue between two committed advocates for their respective faiths.

At the same time, I was fascinated by his sense of being called by God to these various mission situations and by his creativity in witnessing to the Christian faith that claimed him, even in countries where attempting to make converts was forbidden. He tells of an experience early in his time in Somalia, where any proselytization was strictly forbidden. He was enjoying his new work with the Mennonite mission school when he was summoned to the district commissioner's office. The commissioner was upset by a report that some of the students were becoming Christian, and he told Shenk that a full investigation was pending.

David responded, "I will not comment on whether students have become believers in the Messiah [a term the Qur'an uses to describe Jesus]. Only God knows the heart."[25] He promised that the mission school, as a guest of the country, sought to obey its laws. "However," he continued, "I have a problem, and I need your advice. When I first believed in Jesus the Messiah many years ago, the Spirit of God filled me with joy and love. I cannot ignore this gift of God. Occasionally a student comes to me saying, 'I see in you the gift of joy and love. I believe the gift comes from the Christian faith within you. Please explain this faith to me and lead me to become a believer.'" David then asked the commissioner, "What then should I do?" The commissioner responded to continue as he was doing and that there would be no further investigation.[26] Shenk recalls that not only did this experience allow the work of the mission school to continue; it was a trust-building event both for the commissioner and for him.

David describes relationships in which both he and his Muslim friends are so enthused and committed to their faiths and so caring for one another that, if they could, they would convince the person of another faith to become part of their faith community. Shenk speaks of a number of ways to make and deepen relationships so that a Christian witness may be heard. On the surface, these seem like simple, commonsense guidelines. As I read his story, however, I see how slow, demanding, and life-encompassing these guidelines are. He first suggests to "Live with Integrity" and "Keep Identity Clear." In his humanity, he embodied who he was as a follower of Christ and why he was there—in response to God's call. He also urges, "Cultivate Respect," "Develop Trust," and "Practice Hospitality." Not only tend to one's own integrity, but also be respectful, trustful, hospitable, inviting, and accepting of invitations for many conversations over cups of tea and meals.[27] Do this with government officials, religious leaders, groups, and individuals.

Out of the integrity of self and the developed trust, one's witness can include acknowledging and addressing the differences. His next chapters speak of this "Dialogue about the Different Centers" (referring to church and *ummah*, the Islamic community), "Answer the Questions," "Confront the Distortions," and "Consider the Choice: The *Hijrah. The Cross.*"

He addresses four questions Muslims almost always have regarding Christianity: Have the Christian Scriptures been altered? What do you mean Jesus is the Son of God? What is the meaning of the Trinity? And how could the Messiah be crucified? Both Christians and Muslims have distortions of the other's God, Scriptures, and beliefs that need to be acknowledged and confronted if conversation and relationship is to grow.

Shenk goes on to speak of the contrast between the central Islamic event and the central Christian event. The *hijrah* marks the beginning of the Muslim calendar, when Muhammad and his followers went from Mecca to Medina at their invitation for him to become not only prophet but political and military leader. Muslims have told Shenk that "the *hijrah* is the most significant event in the history of the world, because for the first time a prophet of God acquired political and military power sufficient to establish a region obedient to the will of God."[28]

By contrast, Shenk notes that six hundred years earlier, Jesus faced a similar choice. With his growing popularity, people saw him as the promised military-political Messiah and wanted to make him that political leader. But he rejected that, and instead he went to Jerusalem as a servant king on a donkey to face crucifixion. Those two journeys, central events in these respective faiths, point to differences in the faith and communities that have developed since then, and the difference needs to be acknowledged.

This leads Shenk to his chapter "Seek Peace and Pursue It," in which he explores what seeking peace means when yielding to the Marxist regime in Somalia that had taken over the Mennonite property.[29] His concluding chapters are "Partner with the Person of Peace" and "Commend Christ."

Guidance in Witness — An Ecumenical Consultation

I'd like to summarize the other resource that addresses the same questions, though in much briefer form. This ecumenically produced document "Christian Witness in a Multi-Religious World" begins with basic principles: "Acting in God's love," "Imitating Jesus Christ," and "Christian virtues." The virtues one is to embody are "integrity, charity, compassion, and humility, and to overcome all arrogance, condescension and disparagement."[30] They cite Galatians 5:22. Next, they speak of "Acts of service and justice" and "Discernment in ministries of healing." In these sections they offer cautions against exploiting situations of poverty and need by offering allurements for conversion, including financial inducements. Also, in offering healing ministries, they call for "fully respecting human dignity and ensuring that the vulnerability of people and their need for healing are not exploited."[31]

Their next principle is "Freedom of religion and belief," which they describe as including "the right to publicly profess, practice, propagate and change one's religion."[32] When this is denied by any government or exploited by any religion, they call for prophetic witness against such practices. (This is an interesting contrast to Shenk's book, where he describes finding less-confrontational ways to witness even where these liberties are severely curtailed.)

"Mutual respect and solidarity," "Respect for all people," and "Renouncing false witness" are the next three principles. They speak of how to relate to individuals as well as to the cultures in which they find themselves, and also "to acknowledge and appreciate what is true and good in them."[33] The next is "Ensuring personal discernment," which acknowledges that changing one's religion is a big and decisive step with a potential for painful consequences. Adequate time, reflection, and preparation should be encouraged before taking this step.

Their final principle is "Building interreligious relationships," relationships of respect and trust to promote deeper mutual understanding as well as cooperation for the common good. This is the dialogue-conversation aspect, which they encourage at the same time as promoting a respectful witness of service and word, inviting and welcoming converts.[34]

The Enrichment of Conversation

I have summarized both of these writings as part of my discovery that this topic is much more complex than I first thought. These mission leaders write from long experience and collective wisdom. They explore the issues from a wide variety of cultures. Theirs is a global perspective.[35] And yet, as I consider these questions from the perspective of my growing experience in the North American context, I'd like to add a few more considerations.

From the beginning, I have had the sense that whether anybody convinces anybody of anything or not, these conversations are important and mutually spiritually enriching experiences. Whether it was gathering an interfaith committee to plan an event, or visiting with others at a public gathering, or worshipping at a mosque or synagogue and visiting afterwards, I experienced a sense of discovery and enrichment. I met good people, caring people, hospitable and friendly people, and sometimes sacrificial people. They all lavishly contributed their time, labor, and knowledge to help me plan and lead the event for which I had recruited them. I began with a task-centered approach, but we paused to get acquainted, eat meals, and drink tea and coffee together. Our mutual task completed, we had become friends. I could call on them in the future (and have), and they could call on me.

I can remember thinking, "This is not as hard as I thought it would be." And then I had to wonder, why are Christian and Muslim communities so isolated from each other? What could overcome the barriers between us? I realized that this experience of encounter, this community, is so different from the descriptions of Muslims (and sometimes Jews) found on social media and promoted by some religious leaders. Those views are casting shadows on this community and influencing how they are viewed and treated.

Gradually I became aware that my inner life was being enriched and that my believing world was expanding. I hope I was kind and respectful to those I met and that some good came out of our gatherings. The personal enrichment I experienced would have been enough for me to undertake this journey. I will tell you more about that as we continue.

I don't think I have convinced anyone to leave his or her religion and embrace mine, and I still hold to my own faith in Christ with joy and trust. But I delight in and am drawn to further conversations. And so, while I have told you the best things I have discovered about this interfaith conversation or conversion dilemma, it is far from settled for me. We will approach this topic again from a different angle in chapter nine.

Reflect, Discuss, Do

1. This chapter describes the different purposes Christians might have for getting to know persons of other religions. Where were you on this subject when you started reading?

2. After reading and reflecting on this chapter, are you in the same place, or has some change occurred within you? If so, what and why? If not, why not?

3. In what ways are efforts towards conversation and efforts towards conversion related and intertwined?

4. What interfaith conversations are happening in your community? What conversations need to happen?

5. **Do:** Get to know a person of another religion.

Notes

1. Lawrence Kushner, *Jewish Spirituality: A Brief Introduction for Christians* (Woodstock, VT: Jewish Lights Publishing, 2001, 2002), 97–98.

2. Stephen Prothero, *God Is Not One: The Eight Rival Religions That Run the World—and Why Their Differences Matter* (New York: HarperOne, 2010), 18–19.

3. Nabeel Qureshi, *Seeking Allah, Finding Jesus: A Devout Muslim Encounters Christianity* (Grand Rapids: Zondervan, 2014).

4. Ibid., 287.

5. Jerald F. Dirks, *The Abrahamic Faiths: Judaism, Christianity and Islam Similarities and Contrasts* (Beltsville, MD: Amana Publications, 2004), 7–8.

6. Ibid., 9.

7. Ibid., 10.

8. Ibid., 20–21.

9. Shalom Goldman, *Jewish-Christian Difference and Modern Jew-*

ish Identity: Seven Twentieth-Century Converts (Landham, MD: Lexington Books, 2015), 29.

10. Ibid., 28.

11. Ibid., 31.

12. Ibid., 47.

13. Ibid., 54.

14. Ibid., 56.

15. Ibid., 61.

16. Ibid., 69–70.

17. Ibid., 78.

18. Ibid., 90.

19. Aisha Stacey, "Why Do Muslims Call Others to Islam?" August 18, 2014, accessed July 17, 2016, http://www.islamreligion.com/articles/10655/why-do-muslims-call-others-to-islam/.

20. Ibid.

21. World Council of Churches, "Christian Witness in a Multi-Religious World," June 28, 2011, accessed July 26, 2016, https://www.oikoumene.org/en/resources/documents/wcc-programmes/interreligious-dialogue-and-cooperation/christian-identity-in-pluralistic-societies/christian-witness-in-a-multi-religious-world, 3.

22. David W. Shenk, *Christian, Muslim, Friend.: Twelve Paths to Real Relationship* (Harrisonburg, VA: Herald Press, 2014).

23. Ibid., 19.

24. Badru D. Kateregga and David W. Shenk, *A Muslim and a Christian in Dialogue* (Scottdale, PA: Herald Press, 1997).

25. Shenk, *Christian, Muslim, Friend.*, 32.

26. Ibid., 32–33.

27. Ibid., 3–4.

28. Ibid., 126.

29. Ibid., 135.

30. World Council of Churches, "Christian Witness," 3.

31. Ibid.

32. Ibid., 4.

33. Ibid., 3–4.

34. Ibid., 4–5.

35. It is well worth reading and reflecting on either or both of these resources. The WCC document "Christian Witness in a Multi-Religious World" is easy to access. It is brief (5 pages), free, and accessible electronically online (see note 21). David Shenk's book *Christian, Muslim, Friend.: Twelve Paths to Real Relationship* is reasonable, readable, enriched with discussion questions at the end of each chapter, and helpful for both individuals and small groups.

CHAPTER FIVE

Evil Religions, or Evil Possibilities in Each Religion

Why do you see the speck in your neighbor's eye but do not notice the log that is in your own eye? —Matthew 7:3

It is easy to see (or imagine) what's wrong with another's religion—the seeming strangeness, the faults, the blind spots, or even the potentially dangerous aspects. And it is even easier to take the inherent goodness of one's own religion for granted. Where our religion speaks and where it is silent, where it is a force for good and where it is not, where it is prophetic in confronting issues and where it turns away—those aspects of our own religion can be invisible to us or taken for granted.

I have been personally aware of such criticisms—and blind spots— between various Christian groups, particularly Protestant and Catholics, as I mentioned in the Introduction. Now this practice of religious self-justification and criticizing the other is resurfacing with urgency in our interreligious world. I think especially of conversations about Islam, both in the media and in the lives of us everyday folk. While such tensions can and do exist between many religions, for now I will focus on Christianity and Islam.

A Glimpse at Our Muslim Neighbors

Islam is a fast-growing religion, both in the world and in the United States. Its numbers in the United States already exceed that of the Episcopalian and Presbyterian denominations combined. It is the third-largest religious body in our country and may surpass the second (Judaism) in the near future. When persons become aware of the presence of Islamic centers or mosques in their communities, if they are aware at all, they may observe people of varied nationalities and ages gathering for prayer on Fridays and at other times. The members of their congregations—peaceful citizens, students, workers, professionals—are growing and serving in their communities.

All of this is reason enough to want to get to know these relatively new neighbors in the religious community. However, the biggest impetus to learn about Islam seemed to be, above all, the tragic attacks of September 11, 2001, and next, the growth and visible barbarism of the ISIS movement. Given this recent history, we don't often start at the beginning: what do Muslims believe, what is their holy book, how do they practice their faith? Instead, our conversations may start with fear and suspicion—is this a violent, evil religion? Let's look for some handles to engage first our own thinking and then any difficult discussions needed on this sensitive topic.

When Muslims look to their holy book, the Qur'an, for guidance on this question, they find a wide variety of teachings:

• Against killing of the innocent (5:32): "We decreed to the Children of Israel that if anyone kills a person—unless in retribution for murder or spreading corruption in the land—it is as if he kills all mankind, while if any saves a life it is as if he saves the lives of all mankind."

• Against killing in general (17:32): "Do not take life, which God has made sacred."

• Against suicide (2:195): "Spend in God's cause: do not contribute to your destruction with your own hands, but do good, for God loves those who do good."

The Qur'an also offers a variety of teachings about war. These come from a time when Muhammad and his followers were under attack and fighting for their survival. John Esposito wisely reminds us, "Like all scriptures, Islamic sacred texts must be read within the social and political contexts in which they were revealed."[1] In this context the Qur'an provides guidelines and regulations on war: "who should fight (Q 48:17, 9:91), when fighting should end (2:192), how to treat prisoners (47:4)."[2] The emphasis is on proportionality in warfare and guidance for making peace.

Extremist Interpretations of Islam from Within

From early on, Muslims have differed on the interpretation of these teachings about conflicts. If fighting is to be only in defense, what kind of attack justifies defensive warfare? Who are truly living out the teachings of the faith and who are the enemies? Who are apostate, the unfaithful within Islam, from which the rest of Muslims need to be defended? Throughout the history of Islam, the acknowledged (mainstream) leaders have had to overcome extremists from within.

The extremist Islamist groups of recent years—al-Qaeda and now ISIS—interpret themselves as acting in defense of Islam against unjust forces both within the Islamic community and in the West. ISIS aims to correct the false and artificial boundaries created by European forces following World War I that divided the Mideast into various "colonies" of the European nations. They also intentionally fill a gap arising out of the US invasion of Iraq and Afghanistan that destabilized their governments and destroyed their infrastructure. ISIS does this in a world of Arab conflict and separation, particularly the civil war in Syria.

To counter this chaos, ISIS has declared that they are creating a new caliphate (an Islamic state, ruled by a caliph or chief). The first caliphate was under Muhammad. In the new caliphate, they declare, all will live as did the first generation of believers in Islam. Presently, the people have deviated from that ideal. This ideal will be restored in this new caliphate. Their leaders declare an obligation for all to join, and for all who are currently within their influence to give them their absolute, unquestioning loyalty and obedience.

To bring this about in territory they occupy, "ISIS labored hard to remake Mosul [one of the cities it captured and occupied] in its own image. . . . ISIS aimed to rid the city of its history, diversity, cosmopolitanism, and culture, and instead to enforce uniformity and obedience to a harsh set of rules—in short, it created a religious totalitarian system."[3] In the words of Brian Steed, "ISIS sees itself as Holy Warriors of the Light fighting the forces of darkness . . . fighting for God against the godless, offering their followers a cause and a purpose."[4] ISIS leaders have also crafted a skillful social-media campaign, arousing enthusiasm and enlisting volunteers from around the world. The story they tell and the cause they claim to serve has had a lively hearing and response. Concerned parents, Islamic and other, have been fearful that their young adults might be enticed to the adventure and the cause. (Since this chapter was initially drafted, about two years before publication, the situation for ISIS is much changed. There are tremendous reverses in their military fortunes, and they seemed to now be inspiring surprise attacks on unarmed citizens in many places in the world.)

Is such a movement Muslim? Clearly it has connections to and roots in Islam. However, it is far afield from so many others of that faith. ISIS is an extreme and suspect application of the Islamic faith. Author and academic Fawaz Gerges describes a "harsh and selective reading of the scripture" leading to "the instrumentalization of religion for political purposes."[5] In other words, he questions their interpretation of Scripture and sees them as using their religion for their political ends. ISIS is not a widely approved or accepted movement within the Islamic world. I have heard two different speakers state that less than one-tenth of one percent of the world's 1.6 billion Muslims approve of or support ISIS.

As to the ISIS suicide bombers, Croatian author and theologian Miroslav Volf quotes Matthias Kunzel in this regard: "For a Muslim deliberately to be sent to certain death has been considered sacrilege within Islam. . . . The systematic employment of Muslims as guided human bombs with the aim of killing as many people as possible was not seen in the first 1,360 years of Islam, but was invented only 25 years ago."[6]

When and How Any Religion Can Become Evil

Rather than ask if the behavior of a minute minority of people from a given religion makes that religion evil, we should ask what factors can influence religious people to do evil things—people of any religion. Charles Kimball, a professor of comparative religion, explores this question in his important book *When Religion Becomes Evil*. He begins with these poignant observations:

> Religion is arguably the most powerful and pervasive force on earth. Throughout history religious ideas and commitments have inspired individuals and communities of faith to transcend narrow self-interest in pursuit of higher values and truths. The record of history shows that noble acts of love, self-sacrifice and service to others are frequently rooted in deeply held religious worldviews. At the same time, history clearly shows that religion has often been linked directly to the worst examples of human behavior . . . more wars have been waged, more people killed, and these days more evil perpetrated in the name of religion than by any other institutional force in human history.[7]

Kimball asks, when has an otherwise good religion become corrupted? He responds by first citing Jesus' statement in Matthew 22:37-40 to love God with one's whole being and neighbor as oneself. He finds this a universal teaching among religions in their core convictions. A religion has become corrupted, he notes, "when [its] behavior toward others is violent and destructive, when it causes suffering among the neighbors."[8]

Kimball next asks what causes religion to become a force for evil. He answers by listing five factors, any one or any combination of which can contaminate religion from good to evil. When any of these is present, it is all too easy for good, loyal adherents of a religious group to slip into destructive attitudes and behaviors. Understanding the factors as warning signs that lead people of goodwill into destructive ways needs to be a high priority, for it happens all too often.

Absolute Truth Claims

The first warning sign according to Kimball is "absolute truth claims." Every religion has claims about inspiration, God, and truth that the adherents believe. But in healthy religion, "Authentic religious truth claims are never as inflexible and exclusive as zealous adherents insist."[9] However deeply we believe in the claims of our faith tradition, as the apostle Paul put it, we "see in a mirror dimly" and "know only in part" (1 Corinthians 13:12).

Those using absolute truth claims may choose particular texts from their Scriptures, read them selectively (and probably out of context), and then apply them absolutely. For example, a Christian group known as "Army of God" absolutizes such verses as Psalm 106:37 ("They sacrificed their sons and daughters to the demons") and concludes that anything that reduces the death of innocent lives is justified. They deem abortion to be government-sanctioned murder of innocents, and so they support (and effect) the murder of doctors who provide abortions.

Another example: some Muslim leaders take out of context and absolutize a verse from the Qur'an 2:190-191, which says in part, "Fight in the cause of God those who fight you" to justify recruiting and equipping suicide bombers. Their selective, out-of-context, literalist reading justifies the mass destruction of those whom they see as causing their misery.

Whatever the religion, those making absolute truth claims are seen as fundamentalists and Scripture literalists. There is great need, often missing, for dialogue with others within one's own religion and other religions about the whole witness of our Scriptures and how we have embraced the truth that holds us.

Blind Obedience

The second warning sign is "blind obedience." Following the direction and commands of a religious authority uncritically may begin with a charismatic religious leader expounding some new dimension of religious truth and attracting enthusiastic followers. The founder becomes the prime or only religious authority for these followers, who trust their leader and do what the leader says without questioning. This can lead to tragic consequences.

An example from the 1970s is Jim Jones and the Peoples Temple. Jones was a charismatic leader, rooted in Pentecostalism and a commitment to racial integration. His progressive leadership led to his ordination and accreditation of his congregation by the Disciples of Christ denomination. But Jones's behavior became increasingly erratic, and he led his congregation to what was informally named Jonestown in Guyana, South America, and proclaimed himself divine. A congressman and his delegation investigating the congregation were murdered, and shortly thereafter, Jones led his whole group into poison-induced suicide. (Charismatic leaders have also influenced followers to achieve great good in the world. Martin Luther King Jr., for example, was a Christian leader who helped the United States take important strides forward in the civil rights struggle for African Americans.)

Kimball cautions, "Blind obedience is a sure sign of trouble. The likelihood of religion becoming evil is greatly diminished if there is freedom for individual thinking and when honest inquiry is encouraged."[10] Followers have a right and a responsibility to consider and evaluate whatever their leader asks of them.

Ideal Time

The third warning factor involves attempts to predict or establish the "ideal time." This is the belief, found in various forms in Judaism, Christianity, and Islam, that the time is coming soon or is present now for a new, divinely ordered state to come into being. For Jews, this may be the establishment of a third temple on the mount currently occupied by the Muslim Dome of the Rock and Al Aqsa Mosque. For Christians, it may be a new thousand-year reign of God following the battle of Armageddon and the second coming of Jesus. For Muslims, this ideal time may be a new caliphate that recaptures the days of Muhammad's early leadership and the time just after his death. As I have already mentioned, this is exactly what ISIS leaders were claiming for themselves, particularly in the height of their expanded possession of disputed territory.

These views of imminent ideal times are troubling at their best and dangerous at their worst. "Those who narrowly define ideal temporal structures of the state and determine that they are God's agents to establish a theocracy are dangerous. . . . Beware of people and groups whose political blueprint is based on a mandate from heaven that depends on human beings to implement."[11]

The End Justifies Any Means

The fourth warning factor is the belief that "the end justifies any means." Kimball provides examples of several religious groups who espouse worthy goals that sometimes lead to inappropriate actions. One goal of a religious group may be to defend spaces it considers sacred, but this has sometimes led to violence against those who are thought to violate the space (more on this in the next chapter). A religious group may want to reinforce and protect its group identity, but sadly, the means for doing so sometimes has been to denigrate, harass, and persecute those of another religious group, such as some Christian words and actions against Jews that led to inquisitions and too little resistance to the Holocaust. An end may be "reinforcing group identity from within," but to do this, practices denying the dignity and worth of women may be perpetuated. A goal may be "protecting the institution," but to do this, evil deeds may be denied or suppressed, such as the Catholic Church's and other religious groups' failure to respond appropriately to the sexual abuse of children by some clergy.

Kimball calls on us to preserve the connection between the goals of our religions and how they are accomplished. There needs to be unity and harmony of means and ends. He illustrates this by speaking of Mahatma Gandhi, a deeply religious Hindu man. Based on his understanding of religious truth, Gandhi led a nonviolent revolution that ended both British colonial rule of India and challenged the Hindu caste system. But always, Gandhi insisted in unity of ends and means and sought peace both with the British and among the various religious groups of India.

Holy War

The fifth warning sign is a declaration of holy war. This is a modern distortion of religion with ancient roots. In the 1990s and 2000s, Osama bin Laden repeatedly called for *jihad* (holy war) against the United States, Israel, and "infidel" Muslim leaders. Following 9/11, some US leaders spoke of waging a "war on terror."

Christian history reveals three attitudes on war: pacifism, just war, and crusade or holy war. Christians were pacifists for the first three centuries after Christ, and some Christian groups have advocated pacifism ever since. In the fifth century, St. Augustine laid out the principles for just war. These principles included the following: proclaimed by lawful authority; just cause; rightful intention; proper means. Other conditions were also noted, such as protection of non-combatants and reasonable chance of success. Christians have also engaged in holy war. Near the end of the eleventh century, Pope Urban II preached a sermon calling for the First Crusade, in which he said, "You are obligated to succor your brethren in the East menaced by an accursed race, utterly alienated from God. The Holy Sepulcher of our Lord is polluted by the filthiness of an unclean nation."[12]

Raymond of Agiles wrote of that First Crusade's conquest of Jerusalem: "Some of our men (and this was the more merciful) cut off the heads of their enemies; others shot them with arrows . . . Piles of heads, hands and feet were to be seen in the streets of the city . . . men rode in blood up to their knees and the bridle reigns . . . it was a splendid judgment of God . . . it was worth all our previous labors and hardships to see the devotions of pilgrims at the Holy

Sepulcher. How they rejoiced and exulted and sang the ninth chant to the Lord."[13]

Muslims also have need to reconsider the holy war concept. Earlier, we quoted Osama bin Laden using the term *jihad*. His use of this term and the acts he inspired, directed, and praised was Holy War at its worst.

However, the root meaning of "jihad" is "striving" or "struggling in the way of God." Jihad can mean being engaged in war in defense of Islam and of God. The other definition of jihad "is the constant struggle to be virtuous and moral, to do good works on behalf of others and for the betterment of society."[14] Kimball illustrates this by telling of meeting a caring person in Egypt named Dr. Abdeen. She had established a clinic for children with serious, chronic heart problems and told Kimball that this work was her jihad. There is a saying attributed to Muhammad that as they were returning from battle, he told them that they were going to the "greater jihad" from the "lesser jihad."

The idea of holy war is the most pervasive of the ways by which a religion becomes evil. When leaders of nations adopt this religious language and perspective, their citizens, for the sake of patriotism, often go along with it. Thus we repeat the sad history of more wars being fought, people killed, and evil perpetuated in the name of religion than any other institutional force in history. In some way, this very common distortion needs to be held up for questioning. As Kimball concludes, "This much is crystal clear: holy war is not holy."[15]

We have explored Kimball's analysis of five ways religion can become evil: absolute truth claims; blind obedience demanded; ideal time established; belief that the end justifies the means; and declaring holy war. As we evaluate the practices of persons in other religions, I believe that we Christians are called to look at these practices in the light of the word from Jesus with which we started this chapter, "Why do you see the speck in your neighbor's eye but do not notice the log that is in your own eye?" (Matthew 7:3).

As Kimball wisely counsels us, religion has the capacity for doing great good, but it can be corrupted and, thus, both become and cause evil.

Reflect, Discuss, Do

1. What has been your view of the connection between Islam and violence? Of Islam and al-Qaeda and ISIS? What in this chapter has offered you food for thought?

2. As you think about religions you have known or read about, which of the five ways that a religion becomes evil have you observed or read about? From what you know, what was the impact on that religion and its participants?

3. What do you believe about Christianity and war? Are your beliefs closer to pacifism, just war, or holy war?

4. **Do:** If you want to dig deeper into when religion becomes evil, I urge you to read Kimball's book, cited in the notes below. I have provided you the briefest of summaries.

5. **Do:** Interview someone with a different view of Christians and participation in war than you hold. If you'd like to talk with a pacifist, contact a Mennonite, Amish, or Quaker community to find a person with those convictions.

Notes

1. John L. Esposito, *What Everyone Needs to Know About Islam* (Oxford: Oxford University Press, 2002), 119.

2. Ibid., 123.

3. Fawaz A. Gerges, *ISIS: A History* (Princeton: Princeton University Press, 2016), 272.

4. Brian Steed as summarized by Ed Chasteen, personal mailing, in an email that Chasteen circulated.

5. Gerges, *ISIS*, 292.

6. Matthias Kunzel, quoted in Miroslav Volf, *Allah: A Christian Response* (New York: HarperOne, 2011) 286, note 6.

7. Charles Kimball, *When Religion Becomes Evil* (New York:

HarperSanFrancisco, 2001), 1.

8. Ibid., 39.

9. Ibid., 41.

10. Ibid., 99.

11. Ibid., 125.

12. Roland H. Bainton, *Christian Attitudes toward War and Peace* (New York & Nashville: Abingdon Press, 1960), 110–111, as quoted in Kimball, *When Religion Becomes Evil*, 161.

13. Bainton, *Christian Attitudes*, 112–113, as quoted in Kimball, *When Religion Becomes Evil*, 163–164.

14. Ibid., 175.

15. Ibid., 182.

CHAPTER SIX

We All Have Reasons to Repent

As he came near and saw the city, he wept over it, saying, "If you, even you had only recognized on this day, the things that make for peace! But now they are hidden from your eyes."—Luke 19:41-42

The summer I studied in Israel, on one of our days off, several of us visited the Palestinian city of Hebron, located in the West Bank south of Jerusalem. The city is famous as the site where Abraham purchased a cave after Sarah's death to bury her, as described in Genesis 23. Thus the Cave of the Patriarchs is in Hebron, and it is believed that several of the biblical patriarchs and matriarchs are also buried there. Cenotaphs (monuments) honor Abraham, Sarah, Jacob, Leah, Joseph, and Isaac. Supposedly, Adam's footprint can also be found there. Because of its association with Abraham, the city is venerated by Jews, Christians, and Muslims. It is viewed as a holy city by both Islam and Judaism. Indeed, it is the second holiest city for Judaism after Jerusalem.

A building with two distinct parts has been erected over the Cave of the Patriarchs. This building has two entrances. One entrance is to a Jewish synagogue. Only Jewish worshipers may enter. The other entrance is to a Muslim mosque. Only Muslim worshipers may enter. Visitors and tourists of any faith may access either entrance, but only if they adhere to specific religious guidelines. In the synagogue, males are required to wear yarmulkes. Before entering the mosque, all people take off their shoes, and women are provided robes with head coverings.

With visitor status, our group of students (which included one Jew and one Muslim as well as several of us Christians) was allowed to spend time in both spaces. Harmen, our Muslim classmate, was hassled by Israeli soldiers before being allowed to enter the Jewish side. She had bought a fez for her son in the marketplace, and she had to leave it with the soldiers before being allowed to enter.

The name "Hebron" might translate as "union, league, association," but the twentieth-century history and the present city could not fall farther short of such a name. A small settlement of Jews lives in Hebron and is protected by the Israeli military—a situation that has created much tension.

This venerated holy site has had a troubled history. On August 23, 1929, tension between a small Jewish community and the larger Palestinian population exploded, and for three days, Hebron turned into a city of terror and murder. By the time it ended, sixty-seven Jews lay dead, their homes and synagogues destroyed. During this time of terror, some four hundred Jews survived because they were hidden by Arab families. Most of these Jewish survivors were then relocated to Jerusalem.

On February 25, 1994, a radical Jewish settler, Brooklyn-born physician Baruch Goldstein, sprayed bullets into the Ibrahimi Mosque at the Cave of the Patriarchs compound, killing twenty-nine Muslim worshipers outright and wounding 125. He was over-powered, disarmed, and then beaten to death by survivors. The final death toll was probably around 40. Despite efforts by the government of Israel, Goldstein has been revered by many Jews as a martyr, with hundreds visiting his grave each year in homage to him and what he did.

Abraham's cenotaph is situated where both Jews and Muslims may view it. However, one of my classmates pointed out an important detail to me that I would have otherwise missed: The monument is protected by bulletproof glass, so that the violence of the Jewish children of Abraham and the Muslim children of Abraham will not explode again, at least not in this sacred space.

Our Past

Visiting Hebron was a vivid reminder that we all have reasons to repent and seek forgiveness for the ways we have treated one another. This repentance needs to start with acknowledging our history with the other faith community, along with an honest look at our present-day circumstances and conduct.

Some might object, "Why apologize for the past? I wasn't there and did not take part." True, but awareness of our past reminds us that we do not start from a neutral place. We have past hurts and animosities with each other, of which we must be aware. This history may be a part of our present conversation without our even realizing it. Therefore, let's take a brief look at both our past and our present, to see if we need to apologize or not.

Jewish-Christian Relations

The beginning of Jewish-Christian relations starts with Jesus, who among other things was an itinerant rabbi. Amy Levine, a Jewish scholar of the New Testament, summarizes our beginnings aptly:

> Jesus of Nazareth dressed like a Jew, prayed like a Jew (most likely in Aramaic), instructed other Jews on how best to live according to the commandments given by God to Moses, taught like a Jew, argued like a Jew with other Jews, and died like thousands of other Jews on a Roman cross. To see him in first-century Jewish context and to listen to his words with first-century Jewish ears do not in any way undermine Christian theological claims.[1]

After his crucifixion, Jesus' followers experienced appearances of him, resurrected and alive. He was with them from time to time, guided them further, and told them to make disciples of all nations. Seeing Jesus in the light of this transforming experience brought Jesus' followers to a new understanding of who he was—and into conflict with their fellow Jews. This led to vigorous first-century debates. Was

Jesus the messiah promised in the Hebrew Scriptures? Some Jews said no, because that messiah would bring political deliverance; other Jews said yes, that he had transformed the meaning of messiah, combining Isaiah's suffering servant and offering redemption to the nations. Did Jesus rise from the dead, validating all that he had said and done? Some Jews said yes. Other Jews denied this and adhered to the belief that the resurrection will be only on the last day.

While such theological debates were common among Jews in that era (and still are), by the time the New Testament was written, with various books by different authors, it contained some rather harsh descriptions of the Jews. For example, in the Gospel of John, "the Jews" are mentioned seventy-one times, usually in strong opposition to Jesus. The Book of Acts describes Jews resisting and interfering with missionaries reaching out with the message of Jesus to whoever would receive it.

The evidence of conflict between Jews and early followers of Jesus within the New Testament is abundant. How serious is the division? Does difference in belief need to influence how we treat one another? Professor and author Stephen R. Haynes points to varying ways Christians have seen this difference. He speaks of three different views: Reformist, Radical, and Rejectionist.[2]

The Reformist view is that Christian anti-Judaism is seen as "a perennial but alien . . . blight on Christianity. . . . Anti-Semitism . . . is essentially foreign to authentic Christianity."[3] This view sees the conflict as a vigorous family dispute, because as scholars have noted, Christianity began as a kind of Judaism. Thus, from the Reformist perspective, we must recognize that words spoken within a family are inappropriately appropriated by those outside the family.

By contrast, the Radical view is that in the decades after Jesus, the early Christian church understood itself as the "true Israel" and Jesus as the Jewish Messiah. In other words, we are right, and you are wrong. Rosemary R. Ruether, the initial scholar who took this view, contended that anti-Judaism was so basic to this Christian understanding that "it rightly could be called the left hand of Christology."[4] She added that this didn't reflect the teachings of our founder, Jesus.

By further contrast, the Rejectionist view insists that "Christian faith may be inherently as well as historically anti-Jewish."[5] Those with this view see Jewish and Christian scholars having a "failure of nerve" to describe how completely anti-Jewish views are found in Christian literature through the centuries.

Sadly, history does reveal that these disagreements in belief evolved into harsh criticism and treatment. Over the centuries, Jews in the diaspora (living all over the world) had a rather fragile existence. Many factors contributed, perhaps a combination of ethnic prejudice and jealousy when Jews succeeded professionally or financially. This may have been compounded because Jews did not mingle culturally. It must also be said that a good deal of the harsh treatment inflicted on them was generated by religious conflict.

The Jews were expelled from both England and France in the thirteenth century, then sometimes allowed back if they paid large sums of money. The Inquisition, primarily in Spain in the fourteenth and fifteenth centuries, attempted to detect which Jews publicly professed to be Christians while secretly continuing Jewish practices. A decree in 1492 declared that all Jews be baptized or, along with Muslims, deported. The Crusades, though directed at Muslims, also imposed pillage and slaughter on Jews along the way.

Over the centuries, Christian preachers and theologians have used the term *Christoktonon* or Christ killers for the Jews. It was first used by John of Antioch, who was known as Chrysostom or Golden Mouth in the fourth century of the Common Era. For over a thousand years, the Good Friday Mass of the Catholic Church had a series of reproaches, one of which blamed the Jews for killing Christ. This in turn caused fear and dread in the Jewish community every Good Friday. This reproach was finally removed by the reforms of Vatican II.

This is the briefest of summaries of a very sad aspect of our Christian history that led up to an even more tragic one—the Holocaust. The scholars I've read on the possible connection between this pre-history and Germany in the 1930s and 1940s observe that, while there is no direct connection between these teachings and the Holocaust, a closer relationship between Jews and Christians might have resulted in more resistance to Adolph Hitler. When Hitler was asked what he planned to do about the Jews, he said he would do what Christians had been preaching for centuries.

Six million Jews, two-thirds of Europe's Jews and one-third of the world's Jewry, died in that genocide, along with gypsies, Catholics, Jehovah's Witnesses, persons with disabilities, and homosexuals. As Victoria Barnett has noted, while Hitler's intent was clear, he could not have done it by himself.[6] The indifference and sometimes helplessness of the large German populace, much of it Christian, contributed to the genocide. Those tragic years need to be emblazoned on the souls of all of us as we consider how to treat people who may believe differently than we do.

While I was working on this chapter, Holocaust survivor, powerful author, and first chair of the United States Holocaust Memorial Museum, Elie Wiesel, died. Let these words from his book *Night* close this section: "Never shall I forget that night, the first night in camp, which has turned my life into one long night, seven times cursed, and seven times sealed. Never shall I forget that smoke. Never shall I forget the little faces of the children whose bodies I saw turned into wreaths of smoke beneath a silent blue sky."[7]

Christian-Muslim Relations

I will now give you an all-too-brief overview of the complex history of Christian-Muslim relations, drawing primarily from Todd Green's *The Fear of Islam*.[8] Some of the early contacts between Muslims and Christians were military and political. Muhammad was not only the receiver of revelations; he was welcomed as a political and military leader when he and his followers came to Medina. By the time he died in 632, most of the Arab peninsula was under his influence. His successors spread this influence of Islam through military campaigns. In that era, both Christians and Muslims promoted their beliefs partially through empire building, and in that era, the Muslims were much more successful. Within the span of a century, a considerable part of what had been the Christian Roman Empire had come under Muslim control.

As Green notes, fear of conquest dominated the first Christian impressions of Islam. Early Christian authors saw Islam "as a scourge from God to punish Christians for their sins."[9] Only as numbers of Christians converted to Islam did they begin to see it as a religious rival. The views developed from first seeing Muslims as pagans and idolaters to learning more about them through contact and discovering they were monotheists. As Christian scholars learned more about their beliefs, including what they believed about Jesus, they changed their description of Islam to "Christian heresy."

Actually, Christians as well as Jews, on the whole, did not fare too badly under Islamic rule. The Qur'an forbade forcing conversions: "There is no compulsion in religion" (Qur'an 2:256). Christians and Jews were viewed as "People of the Book" and lived with protective status, sometimes paying a tax for this privilege in Muslim lands. In even a brief survey of these early centuries of Christian-Muslim relations, we must mention the eight Christian crusades from the end of the eleventh century to the end of the thirteenth century. The original purpose was to reclaim Jerusalem from Muslim control, and they briefly succeeded. But scholars note that many motives and much hardship, cruelty, and bitterness resulted from those military campaigns. In the previous chapter I quoted an eyewitness account of one of the bloodiest battles. To this day the word *crusade* is a hated term among Muslims.

Occasionally Muslims and Christians collaborated, however. For example, in medieval Muslim Spain, Muslims established close relationships with the Catholic bishops of larger cities, which sometimes led to these Christian leaders holding trusted positions in their Muslim governments. Also, the contributions of Islamic scholars in philosophy and the sciences generated exchange of knowledge and thought between the Islamic and European worlds. Muslim scholars made vast contributions to the preserving and enriching of civilization.

While isolated sympathetic portrayals of Islam existed, more generally "Islam lived on in the European imagination as a religion rooted in deceit, violence, and misogyny."[10] This perspective was influenced by fear of the success of the Islamic empire. When its siege on Vienna failed in 1683, the dominance of Islam and the remaining Muslim stronghold of the Ottoman Empire began to fade.

The next chapter of this history is European colonialism from the late fifteenth through the twentieth centuries. While many civilizations have engaged in colonialism, Europe's era began in 1492 with Columbus's "discovery" and claiming of lands for the Spanish monarchs. Green notes, "By the early twentieth century, much of the Muslim world was subject to European rule."[11]

The mid-twentieth century, following World War II, saw a massive movement to independence for these former colonies. This did not mean the end of European influence; "neocolonialism," which is "the practice of a dominant nation controlling or influencing another country by economic means," remained.[12] Though this is a complex subject, many Muslims blame past and present economic and political struggles on western colonialism and neocolonialism.

While other strongly Muslim countries were achieving their independence, an exception was Palestine, where the State of Israel was founded in 1948 with American and European backing, financing, and military support. Without going into any detailed discussion of this topic for now, we need only note that this was and continues to be another wedge in the relations between Muslims and the West.

The increased contact among the various religions and nations through the last few centuries has led to more detailed knowledge of one another and deeper study of religions and civilizations. A scholarly debate during the 1970s and following became influential in American foreign policy and has affected all of us. The debate was over the concept of the "clash of civilizations," which author Todd Green describes as "the belief that global conflict after the Cold War will result from cultural and civilizational differences, including religious ones, and not economic and ideological differences; the phrase is often invoked to reflect the belief that Islam and the West are bound to be in conflict because of irreconcilable cultural and religious values."[13] The scholars who prevailed and influenced Western leaders were convinced there was such a clash, not only because of any misdeeds by the West. They believed that "the real cause of Muslim animosity toward the West [was] jealousy and humiliation in the light of the dominance of Western civilization."[14] At least for a time, the concept of "clash of civilizations" was deeply influential in U.S. foreign policy.

The latest chapter in this troubled history was the horrific suicidal attacks of September 11, 2001, resulting in massive loss of human life. This was an intentional, evil attack by a cell of terrorists. But was it Islamic? Early on, a number of persons, Muslim and non-Muslim, pled with the US government administration not to call it an attack by Muslims, which implied an organic connection to the beliefs of Islam.

Green points to three troubling assumptions linking Islam and violence, assumptions that need to be examined and questioned. "First, while violence in the name of religion has certainly been a part of Islamic history, Islam does not have a monopoly on violence."[15] A second troubling assumption is whether Islamic teachings play a role in the terrorism. Though religious terminology is used, "the causes of terrorism are more often than not rooted in political and economic grievances."[16] The third troubling but widespread assumption "is that Muslims are either silent about or indifferent to terrorist attacks."[17] That is simply untrue. Though afforded little media coverage, numerous condemnations of terrorist attacks have been made by American Muslim organizations, Muslim international leaders, and scholars. Further, a *fatwa* (a ruling on a point of Islamic law given by a recognized authority) by leading Muslims condemned Osama bin Laden and sanctioned Muslim participation in US military action in Afghanistan.

Again, this is a very brief overview of some of the causes for nations and their citizens—many of whom are members of two kindred and closely related religions—to be at such odds with one another. We now turn from the past to the present.

The Present

Jewish-Christian Relations

As a part of my reflection on reasons to repent in Jewish-Christian relations, I will first go back to my previous brief discussion of the Holocaust of six million Jews. Let's look at it from the American side. There is plenty of accountability and blame to go around. The United States remained rather remote and removed from this humanitarian catastrophe until 1938, when President Franklin D. Roosevelt called for an international conference to facilitate the emigration of refugees from Germany and Austria. They met at the French resort of Evian, but nothing significant came of the conference. The countries offered sympathy but also excuses for why they could not accept more refugees. Of all the nations represented, only the Dominican Republic agreed to accept additional refugees.

In 1939 and again in 1940, the US Senate turned down a bill that would have admitted twenty thousand endangered Jewish refugee children, this even after the widely publicized Kristallnacht (the "night of broken glass") attack on Jewish businesses, synagogues, and people. Also in 1939, the German transatlantic liner, the St. Louis, sailed from Hamburg with 937 passengers, mostly Jews fleeing the Third Reich. They thought they had certificates allowing them to disembark in Cuba, but the certificates had been invalidated. The liner sailed up the eastern coast of the United States, hoping for a presidential executive order allowing them to land, but it never came. They were taken back to their almost-certain fate.

In all this we can find one tiny ray of light: some people risked a great deal to rescue and protect some of their endangered Jewish friends and neighbors. The Yad Vashem museum in Jerusalem has identified those they call "The Righteous of the Nations." These are persons, also known as "Righteous Gentiles," who rendered effort and assistance at some risk to protect Jews without any attempt at proselytizing them. As of 2016, the museum lists 26,120 such persons from forty-seven different nations. A few have since become famous—Oskar Schindler, Raoul Wallenberg, the Danish King Christian X, and Danish people. Most have not. Nevertheless, it is estimated that less than one half of one percent of the population was involved in this courageous activity. Professor and author David Gushee has discovered that approximately one in five of the "Righteous Gentiles" identified specifically religious motives for doing so. Here are some of the motives people mentioned as reasons to take this caring risk:

• A special kinship and love for the Jewish people. "We were brought up in a tradition in which we had learned that the Jewish people were the people of the Lord. . . . We had to save them."[18]

• A Christian ethic of character and virtue including hospitality, tenderheartedness, mercifulness, justice, fairness, courage, fortitude, and love for the stranger.

• The teachings of Scripture. "We were taught the second great commandment, 'You shall love your neighbor as yourself.' So I knew what I had to do."[19] Others cited the parable of the Good Samaritan, the Golden Rule, the final Judgment, and the story of Cain and Abel with its question, "Am I my brother's keeper?"

• Some spoke of achieving theological conviction without intolerance. These persons spoke of hearing Hitler's hate-filled rants and seeing SS officers round up Jews, and they knew they were witnessing the antithesis of their most deeply held convictions.

• Yet others spoke of doing so out of a sense of Christian patriotism. "A certain percentage of them acted to save Jews on the basis of loyalty to national values."[20]

And what about Jewish-Christian relations in the present? Do these "Righteous of the Nations" have anything to say to us in our present time? How are Jews and synagogues being treated now? A recent Pew Research Center's investigation of this question is mostly positive. More than a century after the great migration of Jews to the United States (1880 to 1920), Jews are now mostly an accepted minority. They make up about 2 percent of the American population but have a much larger impact. Jews make up 10 percent of the United States Senate, nearly half of the Supreme Court, and lead major corporations, cities, universities, philanthropies, and arts organizations.

Not all the news is good, however. When Jews were asked, "Have you ever been called an offensive name or snubbed because you are Jewish?" 15 percent said they had. This percentage was higher for Orthodox Jews with their distinctive hair and dress; it was also higher for those under the age of thirty.

The darkest part of the Pew Research Center report had to do with hate crimes. FBI statistics of 2011 reported 771 hate crimes against Jews, the largest of any religious group.[21] In 2016, more than half of the 1,538 hate crimes motivated by religion were directed at Jews.[22] Hate crimes include physical assault, damage to property, vandalism, bullying, harassment, and verbal abuse (including insults, offensive graffiti, and hate mail). These may be aimed at a community and its building or at individuals. In 2014, Kansas City experienced a violent hate crime when Frazier Glenn Miller Jr., a neo-Nazi extremist, fired at the Overland Park Jewish Community Center and Villa Shalom retirement village, killing three. It was a painful reminder of how far some in our country still are from its ideals.

What apologies and changes of behavior does this improving but imperfect reality call for?

Christian-Muslim Relations

Earlier I summarized Todd Green's understanding of the growth of Islamophobia over the centuries. He also points out its presence today. He defines Islamophobia as "hatred, hostility and fear of Islam and Muslims and the discriminatory practices that result."[23]

Green lists eight aspects of Islamophobia, categories that he took from an earlier report by the Runnymede Trust in Great Britain, a race equality think tank founded in 1968 by Jim Rose and Anthony Lester. In a previous chapter, I spoke of one of these aspects of Islamophobia. Here are all eight aspects to reflect on and evaluate for ourselves.

1. Islam as monolithic and static. This is the "notion that Islam lacks both diversity and internal differences and disagreements. In other words, all Muslims are basically the same, holding uniform world views and ideologies. . . . To put the matter starkly, if al-Qaeda [or ISIS] launches violent attacks against Western targets, some might conclude that this is due to an inherent quality in Islam, and that by extension all Muslims are fundamentally the same."[24]

2. Islam as separate and other: "The idea that Islam shares none of the core values found in other religions, particularly Judaism and Christianity or in Western culture. Western values such as respect for religious diversity have no home in Islam."[25]

3. Islam as inferior: The view that "Islam is not only different from but also inferior to the West. Islam is barbaric, irrational, and exists in contrast to the civilized, enlightened, and gender-equal West."[26]

4. Islam as the enemy. "Islam . . . is identified as hostile, violent, and aggressive. Islam is a religion bent on conquest, and, for this reason, there is an inevitable 'clash of civilizations' between Islam and the West."[27]

5. Islam as manipulative: "The assumption that Muslims are objects of suspicion because they are viewed as devious, relying on their religion to give them some strategic, military, or political advantage."[28]

6. Racial discrimination against Muslims justified. This is the assumption that you can tell a Muslim by the color of his or her skin.[29]

7. Muslim criticisms of the West invalidated. In this view, Western critique of Islam is seen as a one-way street.[30]

8. Anti-Muslim discourse as natural. "The [Runnymede] report finally notes that anti-Muslim discourse [can become] so pervasive that even some public figures who ardently fight for tolerance and equal rights for all citizens may express little or no concern for the discrimination felt by Muslims in their midst."[31]

I personally hear the first one—Islam as monolithic and static—most often in conversations. But I also need to ask myself: Am I silent when I hear any of these aspects of Islamophobia being voiced? What can I say in a healing way?

Research has revealed that 48 percent of Muslims have experienced racial or religious discrimination in the last year, more than twice as many as any other religious group in America. From anecdotes I have heard, I suspect this number is much higher for women who are easily identified as Muslim by their hijabs. It is clear that hate crimes are increasing across our country, a large portion of them directed at Muslims individually or at their mosques. There were 307 reported hate crimes against Muslims in 2016, up from 257 in 2015. Past or present, we have ample reasons to repent as a nation and search for new ways of relating.

As I have been writing this chapter, two moving stories of repentance crossed my desk. The first is told in a *New York Times* piece dated July 29, 2016:

In July of 2016, in Krakow, Poland, Pope Francis visited the former concentration and extermination camp at Auschwitz, as had two of his predecessors. While there he paid silent homage to the more than one million victims, mostly Jews, who perished in this camp during the Holocaust. The account continues:

> Right before his visit, Francis told reporters that he 'would like to go to that place of horror without speeches, without crowds.' He said he intended to go 'alone, enter, pray,' adding: 'and may the Lord give me the grace to cry.'
>
> The pope began his visit to Auschwitz—in what is now the Polish town known as Oswiecim, about 30 miles west of Krakow—by meeting 12 survivors of the camp. He greeted them, one by one, mostly in silence, expressing his sorrow and respect just by clutching their hands, looking into their eyes and kissing them tenderly, once on each cheek. . . .
>
> The Pope visited the infamous Block 11 where Nazi guards tortured prisoners. While there he stopped at the cell where

Rev. Maximilian Kolbe, a Polish Franciscan friar, had been imprisoned. In 1941 Father Kolbe volunteered to die in place of a stranger and was canonized in 1982. Francis prayed in that cell for some time.

Before leaving, he signed the Auschwitz guest book, writing in Spanish, "Lord, have mercy on your people. Lord, forgive so much cruelty."

Francis met with a group of Polish Catholics who have been recognized by Yad Vashem, the Holocaust remembrance center in Jerusalem, as 'righteous among the nations,' for having risked their lives to save Jews during the Holocaust. . . .

Rabbi [David] Rosen added: 'Francis has been saying all along that it is impossible to be a Christian and an anti-Semite. His visit in Auschwitz is an enormous message of solidarity with the victims and affirmation of his unequivocal reprehension of anti-Semitism and all other forms of racism.'"[32]

The second story of repentance involves Muslims' response to the slaying of a French priest, Father Jacques Hamel, as reported in *Aljazeera*.

Muslims have attended Catholic Mass in churches around France in solidarity and sorrow following the brutal murder of a priest in an ISIL-linked attack. There were more than 100 Muslims among the 2,000 who gathered at the cathedral of Rouen. This was in close proximity to the Normandy town where two teenagers slit the throat of 85-year-old Father Jacques Hamel. "I thank you in the name of all Christians," Rouen Archbishop Dominique Lebrun said in his welcome. He continued, "In this way you are affirming that you reject death and violence in the name of God."

Imam Otaman Aissaoui of Nice led a delegation to a Catholic Mass in that southern city where Mohamed Lahouaiej Bouhlel carried out a rampage in a truck on Bastille Day, claiming 84 lives and injuring 435. There were many Muslims among his victims. "Being united is a response to the act of horror and barbarism," [the Imam] said.

The Notre Dame church in southwestern Bordeaux also welcomed a Muslim delegation, led by the city's top Imam Tareq Oubrou.

'It's an occasion to show [Muslims] that we do not confuse Islam with Islamism, Muslim with jihadist,' said Reverend Jean Rouet.

The Muslims were responding to a call by the French Muslim council CFCM to show their 'solidarity and compassion' over the priest's murder on Tuesday.

'I'm a practicing Muslim and I came to share my sorrow and tell you that we are brothers and sisters,' said a woman wearing a beige headscarf who sat in a back pew at a church in central Paris. Giving her name only as Sadia, she added softly: 'What happened is beyond comprehension.'"[33]

May God have mercy on us all and lead each of us to the things that make for peace.

Reflect, Discuss, Do

1. What in this chapter was new information for you? What do you want most to remember from this chapter? Where, if anywhere, did you feel I was mistaken or ill-informed?

2. You may have noticed that except for the very last story, I have spoken only of our need to repent and apologize to persons in the two religions, Judaism and Islam. Where, if anywhere, do you as a Christian want apologies?

3. In the light of this history, what steps do we need to take to increase interreligious dialogue and understanding?

4. **Do:** If you are ever in Washington, DC, visit the United States Holocaust Memorial Museum or if in Philadelphia, PA, visit the

National Museum of American Jewish History or if in New York City, NY, visit the Center for Jewish History.

5. **Do:** If you have friends or acquaintances of other religions, inquire about their experience. Do they feel safe? Have they been harassed? Is their community and place of worship free of vandalism or threat?

Notes

1. Amy Levine, *The Misunderstood Jew: The Church and the Scandal of the Jewish Jesus* (New York: HarperOne, 2006), 51.

2. Stephen R. Haynes, "Changing Paradigms: Reformist, Radical and Rejectionist Approaches to the Relationship between Christianity and Antisemitism," *Journal of Ecumenical Studies,* Winter, 1995, vol. 32, no. 1, 63–88.

3. Ibid., 65.

4. Ibid., 67–68.

5. Ibid., 71.

6. Victoria Barnett, lecture at United States Holocaust Memorial Museum, June 18, 2008.

7. Elie Wiesel, *Night* (New York: Hill & Wang, 1960), 32.

8. Todd Green, *The Fear of Islam: An Introduction to Islamophobia in the West* (Minneapolis: Fortress Press, 2015).

9. Ibid., 45.

10. Ibid., 65.

11. Ibid., 70.

12. Ibid., 73.

13. Ibid., 90.

14. Ibid., 91.

15. Ibid., 122.

16. Ibid., 123.

17. Ibid., 124.

18. David P. Gushee, "Learning from the Christian Rescuers: Lessons for the Churches," *The Annals of the American Academy of Political and Social Science,* November, 1996, 548, accessed August 12, 2016, http://www.jstor.org/stable/1048549, 142.

19. Ibid., 149.

20. Ibid., 152.

21. Lauren Markoe, "American Jews on Anti-Semitism: Discrimination against Muslims, Gays, and Blacks Worse," *Huffington Post*, October 25, 2013, accessed August 10, 2016, http://www.huffington post.com/2013/10/25/american-jews-anti-semitism_n_4159295.html.

22. http://wqad.com/2017/11/14/fbi-surge-in-hate-crimes-reported-in-2016, accessed November 21, 2017.

23. Green, *The Fear of Islam*, 9.

24. Ibid., 12–13.

25. Ibid., 13–14.

26. Ibid., 14.

27. Ibid., 15.

28. Ibid., 15–16.

29. Ibid., 17.

30. Ibid.

31. Ibid., 19.

32. Joanna Berendt, "Pope Francis, Visiting Auschwitz, Asks God for the 'Grace to Cry,'" *New York Times*, July 29, 2016, accessed August 1, 2016, http://www.nytimes.com/2016/07/30/world/europe /pope-francis-auschwitz.html?_r=0.

33. "Muslims pray with Catholics over French priest's murder," *Aljazeera*, July 31, 2016, accessed August 1, 2016, http://www.al jazeera.com/news/2016/07/muslims-pray-catholics-french-priest-mur der-160731131924563.html.

CHAPTER SEVEN

Questions, Critiques, and Misunderstandings

If it is possible, so much as depends on you, live peaceably with all. ——Romans 12:18

Call upon the way of thy Lord with wisdom and beautiful exhortation, and hold discourse with them [the People of the Book, that is, Jews and Christians] in the finest manner. —Qur'an 16:125[1]

Any relationship, if it is to endure, must go through a number of phases in its development. The first step is meeting. Then can come the delightful step of finding things in common, hearing each other's stories, and realizing how much you have in common. But then differences, limits, and perhaps conflicts emerge. If the relationship is to endure, the participants must work through this stage, asking such questions as: What can I live with? What can I not tolerate? What am I willing to change? Where can we go with this relationship? If the participants can successfully make it through this stage, the relationship has potential to grow into something deep and rich.

This process is necessary for building interreligious relationships as well. It might be slow because we come to such relationships with baggage that includes history, past experiences, impressions, and teachings. Acknowledging our differences, raising our critiques, and hearing the other's critiques is a necessary step. Because we are at so many different places on this journey, what for one person may be a question about something unknown may be a misunderstanding for another or a strong conflict for someone else. Below I will explore a few topics where I have stumbled or others have stumbled with me. You may have a different list on which you need to work.

But first, what are some ground rules that will facilitate such conversations? I personally hope for the willingness to let each person speak of one's own heritage on one's own terms. I also hope for the openness to hear differences and critiques, and for all of us to live with the differences. Conflicts may arise over differences of beliefs or practices.

I remind you that we already devoted chapter five to a discussion of the possibility of violence and other evil in religions. We will let that stand and not return to that specific topic in this chapter. But we can find plenty of other topics that might reveal any misunderstandings between us. Let's consider a few.

Questions about the Meaning and Extent of Religious Freedom

Several years ago Muslim leaders and scholars issued the document "A Common Word between Us and You" to the world faith communities, inviting them to dialogue about a common commitment to what Christians acknowledge as the two great commandments: love of God and love of neighbor.

Among the various world Christian communities, the leaders of the Baptist World Alliance wrote a response in which they expressed appreciation and concurrence with many things, but raised two issues for further discussion. One of those issues was religious freedom. They wrote, "We are impressed by the case you advance for religious freedom. . . . As Baptist Christians, we have always defended the right of religious freedom for all people, regardless of their religion, grounding this theologically in the sovereignty of God."[2]

They then went on to ask what the content and extent of the freedom was to which the document referred. "It seems to us that you are directing your argument in the first place to a defence [sic] of the right of Christians, Muslims and Jews to practice freely the religion in which they have been born, or which they already hold—'to follow what God has commanded them.' This is obviously of critical importance."[3] But then they continued:

> It is not altogether clear to us whether you think that this principle can also cover the freedom of people to change their religion, or to move from a community of one faith to another of a different faith. As Baptist Christians, we believe that the same principle of accountability to the sovereign God gives freedom to make such a change, from Christianity to Islam or from Islam to Christianity.[4]

These scholars are identifying two different views, or perhaps degrees, of religious freedom. One is the freedom to continue in the religious faith into which one was born. The other is the freedom to witness, evangelize, to invite others into one's faith, and to make a change if one feels led under the sovereignty of God.

When I served briefly as a volunteer missionary and guest of the Evangelical Church of Kalimantan on the island of Borneo in Indonesia (a Muslim-majority nation), I learned what it was like to live under that first definition of religious freedom. Christians there were allowed to believe and practice their faith and maintain their religious organizations. However, they could not proselytize—try to convince another to accept their faith. Permission to build a church was given only after a long and difficult process. No identifying sign could be put outside. Mixed Muslim-Christian marriages were not allowed, so when a Muslim and a Christian married, their marriage was considered Muslim and the Christian partner was expected to convert. The Indonesian Christians seemed to thrive much better in that atmosphere than I would have.

In countries where Muslims or any other group are a minority, they live by the laws of that land, as do American Muslims. In many parts of the world, this question of the definition and extent of religious freedom is an issue between Christians and Muslims.

Issues Regarding Women and Men

What are our differences and similarities in how women and men are regarded in our religions and practices? It is important to note that religious practices are deeply influenced by culture and so may vary from country to country.

Do women and men worship together or apart? They sit together in most Protestant and Catholic Christian congregations and in Reform and Conservative Jewish congregations in the United States. They sit separately in Christian groups such as conservative Mennonite and Amish, Orthodox Jewish congregations, and during Muslim times for worship and prayer. The reason I have heard Muslims give for separating at their community prayer times is rather practical: one of the prayer postures is kneeling with one's forehead on the floor, which means one's posterior is in the air. For most modesty and reverence reasons, both genders prefer worshiping segregated by gender. At the same time, there are many variations of preference and practice.

How does each religion refer to the Divine? What language is used for God? After centuries of referring to God as male, many Jews and Christians are finding within their own Scriptures numerous reasons for a female frame of reference for God as well. A few examples are these: "Womb mercy," the Hebrew Bible term for God's mercy; the Wisdom of God as feminine in Hebrew; Spirit as feminine; Jesus comparing himself to a mother hen with her brood; and more. In Islam, Muhammad reportedly said that Allah has ninety-nine names. While some have divided this list into feminine names of beauty and masculine names of majesty, Muslims in general worship a deity who is beyond gender.[5]

Are women allowed to serve in leadership roles or to officiate at worship in a mixed group of both women and men? In most expressions of Islam, Roman Catholicism, Eastern Orthodoxy, conservative Protestant evangelicalism, and Orthodox Judaism, the answer is no. Within Conservative and Reform Judaism and mainline Protestant groups, yes. Acceptance of women's leadership in worship has been a recent development, historically speaking, with a good many changes initiated less than a century ago.

My Muslim friends tell me there are a few places where female imams have been accepted, although this is extremely rare. However, traditions of female leadership are upheld in many aspects of the life of a mosque. They also refer to Aisha, one of Muhammad's wives, who was a scholarly and inquisitive woman who contributed to the spread of Muhammad's message for forty-four years after his death. She was the provider of many *hadiths* (sayings or stories of Muhammad) and was sought as a teacher by both women and men.

Why do many Muslim women wear different clothes—hijabs or burqas—with variations from culture to culture? As explained to me, for two reasons: to emphasize the person and not the appearance, and for reasons of modesty. Many revealing Western clothing styles are not considered appropriate.

Are Muslim women allowed to be educated? in coeducational settings? to be employed in public settings, vote, and hold public office? Yes, widely if not universally, to all of these. As a matter of fact, in the United States, Muslim women generally are better educated than the female population at large. Further, four of the five most populous Muslim-majority countries—Indonesia, Pakistan, Bangladesh, and Turkey—have elected women to their highest political offices.

The Meaning of Some Terms That Occasion Fear or Suspicion

Certain words associated with Islam arouse fear and suspicion and, I have learned, misunderstanding. Let us take a deeper look at two of those words.

Jihad

To continue an earlier exploration, what does the word *jihad* mean? The word can be translated as "struggle," and it has a twofold meaning. It can mean pious striving, such as charity and religious striving. Indeed, the Qur'an commands Muslims to struggle in the path of God

93

and follow the example of Muhammad and his early companions. Thus, a part of the meaning is to struggle within against evil.

Jihad can also refer to a military struggle. Some say it was originally intended to mean only defensive struggles to save one's faith community or society from attack, though others have used it for both defensive and offensive struggles. The term *jihad* is multidimensional. It speaks of the struggle of the soul as well as struggle against those who defeat or destroy what one holds dear. It does not mean the wanton, suicidal, indiscriminate attacks carried out in recent times by Islamic extremists.

The Qur'an speaks of war and regulates war. It speaks of fighting "though it is hateful to you" (Qur'an 2:216). It condemns suicide (4:29). The Qur'an also condemns mass murder, including of women and children (5:32). From the seventh century on, it has been Islamic law and practice to protect the rights of noncombatants.[6]

As with any widespread and historic religion, we can find a variety of opinions and attitudes. And some do indeed employ the word *jihad* for aggressive action against an enemy. I was touched by a blog written by Farouk A. Peru during Ramadan, in which he reflected with sadness on three violent Muslim-on-Muslim attacks in the previous week. He wrote, "I try to ask myself why would young Muslims allow themselves to be drawn to Jihadism? Jihadism . . . is incredibly self-destructive. Why would people with their lives ahead of them allow themselves to be sucked into this abyss of hate and end their lives prematurely?"[7] He then answers his own question, "I believe it is because Jihadism gave them a life purpose. Yes, it is no doubt a perverted life purpose from Islam, in my understanding. Yes, it is evil and should ring warning bells in one's mind. But it is something Traditional Islam has failed to give them—a clear life purpose."[8] He goes on with a plea to expand the teaching of the young to explore, discover, and act on worthier life purposes including civic involvement and responsibility.

From another perspective, Christian campus minister Morgan Guyton wrote a blog called "Three Islamic Concepts I Wish Christians Would Adopt." One of these is jihad. He notes, "What [jihad] means literally is 'struggle' and it's usually taken to mean a struggle against injustice... [or] a struggle against your own idolatry. . . . What if every congregation had to decide every year as part of their strategic planning what social justice in our community would be their jihad for the year? Imagine if Christians were most known to be people who struggle against injustice rather than people who want special privileges for ourselves like tax exemption and the right to discriminate?"[9]

What is jihad? The answer, we discover, is complex. As these last two authors point out, among other things it is an invitation to explore the deeper purposes of the religion we practice.

Sharia Law

What about *sharia*? "Sharia" means the "right path." A few legislatures in the United States have passed bills to prohibit sharia from becoming the law of their state, and politicians have warned against it. Sharia is basically the prescribed path for Muslims for all walks of life, both sacred and secular: family, society, economics, politics, ritual, ethics, and more. Fatina Abdrabboh is the executive director of the American Muslim and Minority Advocacy League (AMAL), a civil-rights organization dedicated to defending against Islamophobia and other forms of racism. Formerly a professor, she relates that a difficult part of teaching a course on sharia is to help students discover what sharia is not. It is not a substitute for civil law, not a book of statutes, not a collection of judicial decisions. Rather it is a body of Qur'an-based guidance for living. Abdrabboh notes that "what sharia means can differ widely from one Muslim to another. It can mean being honest and true to one's self, feeding and helping the poor, combating income inequality, or engaging in reflective prayer." Rather than being a single volume, she continues, "the system of laws that Muslims abide by is a result of a millennium-and-a-half of differing philosophical ideological and political histories of the Islamic world."[10]

Sharia, one might say, constitutes the values by which Muslims live out of the richness of their religious tradition. In Abdrabboh's words, it is "the overarching ideological framework that Muslims live their lives by . . . a set of moral values that, at the end of the day, are ways that help you become a better person, a better community member, and a better citizen."[11]

The Views of Jesus in Other Faith Religions

For us Christians, it is important to know how persons of other faith traditions view Jesus. In the light of that answer, we then know more about where to go in the rest of our conversation.

The Jewish view of Jesus is rather straightforward. They affirm that he was a Jewish teacher-rabbi living during the Roman occupation of Israel in the first century CE. The Romans executed him along with many other religious Jews for speaking out against the Roman authorities and their abuses. Jews did not and do not believe that Jesus was the messiah prophesied in Hebrew Scriptures.

As I have acknowledged, much conflict and harsh treatment have taken place because of the differing beliefs about Jesus between Christians and Jews. In recent years, we have seen some growth in the understanding that differences in belief should not lead to anti-Semitism. In addition, we have learned that we share much in common, from our Hebrew Bible heritage to our shared commitment to a just and peaceful world.

Christians, as I assume you know, believe that Jesus was a first-century teacher-rabbi who was raised from the dead by God after being crucified, and that this event initiated a new faith and way of life for Christ-followers. We see everything from that perspective. We believe that Jesus' crucifixion was an act of love for the healing and forgiveness of all of us. We believe with Paul that "in Christ, God was reconciling the world to himself" (2 Corinthians 5:19). Over the centuries, theologians have pondered and guided us on how humanity and divinity met in this person of Jesus, whom the Nicene Creed affirms is "very God of very God . . . and [who] was made man." We do not cut ourselves off from conversation and religious dialogue with the rest of humankind. But this is where we start, what we believe, and whom we follow.

What do Muslims believe about Jesus? Islam began in a world that had a good deal of knowledge of Judaism and Christianity. Islam, which considers itself the heir (and completion) of the biblical prophets and their revelations, was birthed with the life of Muhammad (570–632, CE) in Arabia. Some Christians and Jews lived among the peoples of his land at that time, so the people would have had some knowledge about Jesus. Perhaps the New Testament Gospels were available, along with the Hebrew Bible and some extrabiblical writings. And while we should remember that Muhammad was illiterate, the revelations-recitations that he received through the angel Gabriel in the Qur'an included words about Jesus.

R. Marston Speight, former director of the Office on Christian-Muslim Relations in the National Council of Churches of Christ in the USA, relates an encounter from the early history of Islam. As Muhammad was drawing his first followers, they faced much opposition and danger. Fearful for the safety of his followers, Muhammad sent about a hundred of them to seek temporary refuge in Ethiopia under a Christian king. When they arrived in Ethiopia, they were taken to the royal presence. The question was put to them: "What do you believe about Jesus?" The spokesman for the group responded, "We say about Jesus that which our prophet told us (may peace be upon him): Jesus is the servant and messenger of God, the spirit and word of God whom God entrusted to the Virgin Mary." Thereupon the king took a stick from the ground and responded, "I swear, the difference between what we believe about Jesus, Son of Mary, and what you have said does not exceed the width of this stick." And they were provided asylum for the time they needed it.[12]

When we explore what the Qur'an says about Jesus, we find that Jesus holds a significant and unique place in Islam. Jesus is mentioned in fifty-nine verses of the Qur'an (Muhammad in only five). Jesus' virgin birth is affirmed (Q 3:45-47), and some of his miracles are described. It is taught that neither Jesus nor Muhammad came to change basic belief in one God (Q 5:46). The Qur'an refers to Jesus as a "Word" from God and a "Spirit" from God and as "Messiah."

Within its pages are pronouncements on his humanity, servanthood, and place in the prophetic line.

In the Qur'an's teaching, however, Jesus is not crucified. His enemies planned it, but God would not allow it. In short, Jesus is held in high regard in the Qur'an but he is "cleansed" (a word used in the Qur'an) of some of the views of him from his own community. And so Jesus is seen in the Qur'an as a unique prophet of gentleness, compassion, and humility.

But there is more. I was pleasantly surprised to learn that the influence of Jesus on Islam does not end with the words of the Qur'an. Palestinian historian Tarif Khalidi has written a book on some three hundred sayings about Jesus or ascribed to Jesus in various Islamic writings over a thousand years of Islamic history. Why did he undertake this study? "[My] aim is primarily to introduce an image of Jesus little known outside Arabic Islamic culture. It is an image that might be of interest to those who wish to understand how Jesus was perceived by a religious tradition which greatly revered him but rejected his divinity."[13] Khalidi collected these sayings and comments on them in his book. Where did he find the sayings? In works of ethics and popular devotion, books of literature, collections of Sufi mysticism, and anthologies of wisdom. He calls this body of literature "The Muslim Gospel."[14] It is fascinating to read this collection of sayings about Jesus from a different religion, culture, and era. Many of them are stories or quotes from the Gospels, but in another setting and often with a different application from the original.

Khalidi also collected some fascinating sayings that, though they must have come from someone else, are attributed to Jesus. One says, "God likes his servant to learn a craft . . . and God hates a servant who acquires religious knowledge and then adopts it as a craft."[15] Many of the sayings advocate asceticism or simplicity. Others refer to talks with Satan (sometimes a disguised Satan), as well as talking with the dead and related discussion of death and judgment.

Over the centuries, a series of images of Jesus emerges: ascetic saint; lord of nature; miracle worker; healer; social and ethical role model. The Sufi mystics solidly embraced Jesus, perhaps more deeply the

Jesus of the Synoptic Gospels (Matthew, Mark, and Luke) than had others before them.

Khalidi draws conclusions that are vital to the questions we are pursuing. In this literature, molded in an Islamic environment, Jesus is always seen as an Islamic prophet. He is portrayed in activities of Islamic piety, reading the Qur'an, praying in an Islamic manner, and going on pilgrimage to Mecca. But Jesus is also seen as challenging that role, stretching it, redefining it. Furthermore, Khalidi notes, the high regard Islamic writers over the centuries expressed for Jesus speaks of the importance of the Muslim gospel for the study of comparative religion. Regardless of the accuracy of these portrayals of Jesus, this is an unusual way "in which one religion reaches out to borrow the spiritual heroes of another religion in order to reinforce its own piety."[16] This in turn may tell us something about how religious cultures interact with one another, learn to coexist, and are mutually enriched in so doing.

This leads Khalidi to an important conclusion: The process of interaction—one religion appropriating the central religious figure of another—points to something else, which is "the need of Christianity and Islam . . . for complementarity." Jesus is a towering figure who "rises above two religious environments, the one that nurtured him and [the] other that adopted him." In this day of much interreligious tension, it's good to note the times when these religions were "more aware of and reliant on each other's witness." In this understanding of Jesus, "he ceases to be an argument and becomes a living and vital moral voice, demanding to be heard by all who seek a unity of profession and witness."[17]

Thanks to this gifted scholar, we can gain a new perspective on how Muslims historically viewed Jesus and how that might impact our understanding of Muslim-Christian relations in our modern age.

Reflect, Discuss, Do

1. What does religious freedom mean to you? How important is it to you? Do you see other religions contributing to or threatening your religious freedom? Why or why not?

2. What is important to you about religious customs and practices regarding women and men?

3. What did you learn and what more would you like to know about the following?

a. Jihad

b. Sharia

4. How should we Christians relate to those who hold a different view of Jesus than we have?

5. **Do:** Have a conversation with someone of another religion about the similarities and differences between their religion and yours.

6. **Do:** Learn more about any interfaith organizations active in your community.

Notes

1. Reza Shad-Kazemi, trans., "Introduction," *My Mercy Encompass All: The Koran's Teachings on Compassion, Peace and Love* (Berkeley: Counterpoint, 2007), 55.

2. Royal Aal al-Bayt Institute for Islamic Thought, Jordan, "ACommonWord-Baptist-World-Alliance-Response.pdf," *The ACW Letter / A Common Word / Christian Responses*, December 28, 2008, accessed September 24, 2016, www.acommonword.com/category/site/christian-responses/

3. Ibid.

4. Ibid.

5. Stephen Prothero, *God Is Not One: The Eight Rival Religions That Run the World—and Why Their Differences Matter* (New York: HarperOne, 2010), 37.

6. Ibid., 34–35.

7. Farouk A. Peru, "Jihadism Gave Terrorists What Muslims Failed To: A Life Purpose," *Personal Al-Islam: A Muslim writes on humanity through the world of Islam* (blog) *Patheos: Hosting the Conversation on Faith*, July 4, 2015, accessed September 5, 2016, http://www.patheos.com/blogs/personalislam/2016/07/jihadism-gave-terrorists-what-muslims-failed-to-a-life-purpose/.

8. Ibid.

9. Morgan Guyton, "On Jihad: Three Islamic Concepts I Wish Christians Would Adopt," *Patheos: Hosting the Conversation on Faith*, December 14, 2015, accessed September 9, 2016, http://www.patheos.com/blogs/mercynotsacrifice/2015/12/14/three-islamic-concepts-i-wish-christians-would-adopt/.

10. Fatina Abdrabboh, "On Shariah Law: Tolerance Is the Law of the Land," *Patheos: Hosting the Conversation on Faith*, July 24, 2016, accessed September 13, 2016, http://www.patheos.com/blogs/altmuslim/2016/07/on-shariah-law-tolerance-is-the-law-of-the-land/?utm_source=SilverpopMailing&utm_medium=email&utm_campaign=Patheos%20072916%20(1)&utm_content=&sp-MailingID=51937815&spUserID=NDEwMTQ5ODA4NzYS1&spJobID=964123006&spReportId=OTY0MTIzMDA2S0.

11. Ibid.

12. R. Marston Speight, *God Is One: The Way of Islam* (New York: Friendship Press, 1989), 1.

13. Tarif Khalidi, ed. and trans., *The Muslim Jesus: Sayings and Stories in Islamic Literature* (Cambridge: Harvard University Press, 2001), 3.

14. Ibid.

15. Ibid., 119.

16. Ibid., 44.

17. Ibid., 45.

CHAPTER EIGHT

Building Understanding by
Serving Side by Side

When the Messiah comes, it may be for the first or the second time. Until then, there is much we can do together.
—Rabbi Alan Cohen

Well before I was beginning my spiritual search on interreligious topics, an exciting movement was making important discoveries and contributions to religious pluralism in North America and beyond. A key catalyst in this movement is the Interfaith Youth Core, whose founder and executive director is Eboo Patel.

Patel is an American Muslim who was born in India. He recalls his adolescence in America as a "series of rejections" based on various aspects of his tradition. Could the multiple dimensions of his heritage—American, Indian, and Muslim—coexist in the same being? For a time it seemed not. In college, however, he discovered that his heroes were people of deep faith. These included Dorothy Day, the Dalai Lama, Martin Luther King Jr., Mahatma Gandhi, Malcom X, and the Aga Khan. They held differing faith traditions, but interreligious cooperation had been a central characteristic of each. Further still, these heroes assumed leadership at an early age.[1]

This led Patel to a flurry of activity over the next several years: exploring through study, teaching in an intercity school, having conversations with friends, attending interfaith conferences, and participating in interfaith service events (which he discovered were happening all over the world). Out of his experiences and conversations with many wise and experienced leaders, Patel and his colleagues launched the Interfaith Youth Core (IFYC) in his home city of Chicago.

Patel said, "We started the organization with two big ideas: that young people should be a priority, not an afterthought, in interfaith cooperation, and that social action should be central to interfaith efforts—enough already with the documents and ceremonies."[2] Patel and other leaders of the IFYC noted that religious extremism was effectively recruiting a movement of young people taking action to the danger of the world. Therefore, a strong alternative was needed that was recruiting for constructive purposes. Patel and his colleagues aspired to provide that.

As the mission grew clearer, from the beginning to the present, IFYC was built on three pillars: intercultural encounter, social action, and interfaith reflection.[3] Patel noted that there was some precedent for their efforts. A number of largely private colleges on the East Coast had developed programs in which a chaplain or professor initiated classes and opportunities for interfaith conversations. This was a niche market of "interested students at elite schools." However, the question Patel asked was, "How to go from niche to norm?"—that is, from engagements of small groups of interested students to high expectations across entire institutions.[4]

As IFYC explored this question, they took note of professor Diana Eck's distinction between diversity and pluralism. Simply put, diversity is people of different backgrounds living in close proximity. Baghdad, Belfast, and Bosnia are all diverse, and each has had serious interreligious violence. Diversity is a fact, but violence doesn't need to be the outcome. Pluralism is an achievement. Eck explains that pluralism "means deliberate and positive engagement of diversity . . . building strong bonds between people from different backgrounds."[5] The grand goal of IFYC was to make religious pluralism a social norm within a generation.

IFYC's work began in Chicago with two basic aspects. One was an interfaith youth council comprising a small number of youths from different faith traditions who met weekly. They were asked to honor their own traditions but also to explore what each of their faiths contributed to the values they held in common. These values included mercy, compassion for the poor, care for the environment, and hospitality. The members of the youth council also engaged in social-service projects, partnering with someone from another faith.

The second aspect engaged a much larger population through an annual Interfaith Youth Service Day. Young adults from various faith traditions would be invited to take part. A service project would have work opportunities for all who came, perhaps cleaning up a neighborhood or a river or stream basin. The day would conclude with reflections and discoveries together in small groups of persons from the various faiths participating.[6]

This interfaith movement can teach us a number of lessons. For now, the takeaway on which I will focus is on what is gained, both for our own spiritual self-awareness and for deepening relationships with those of other faiths, when we work together on something that matters and serves our communities. Our faith is further enhanced when each participant identifies and shares what religious teachings led us to that involvement.

IFYC offers many examples. Students from Ohio University cleaned up a waterway. Students at Augustana College in Rock Island, Illinois, held a "Thanksgiving Fast-a-thon" to raise money for a homeless shelter. At other universities, students have organized blood drives, interfaith dinners, campaigns against sexual violence, academic tutoring for struggling students, and help for homeless youth. All these projects included times of reflection during which participants who had worked side by side listened to one another as they explained their religious beliefs and motivations.

Patel tells one story about Greg Damhorst, a student at the University of Illinois. An evangelical Christian who believed his faith is the only way to God, Greg also believed that to follow in the steps of Jesus is to be in right relationship with the world, including persons of other faiths. So he participated in both the Evangelical Christian

Association and the Interfaith in Action activities on his campus. In fact, he became the leader for the weekly shared values discussion and the annual service day of the latter organization. Both these events were quite small for a number of years, though respect for who they were and what they were doing grew.

When the catastrophic earthquake hit Haiti in January 2010, killing thousands and leaving a million people homeless, Greg and his friends found a practical way to help: packing nutritious dry-goods meals. They set a goal to pack a million meals for Haiti in a weekend. Directors of local social-service agencies helped them find a room large enough for the project. One agency helped them get a government grant to pay for the food. With exquisite cooperation and coordination, more than five thousand people packaged over a million meals in a twelve-hour period. They pasted butcher paper on the wall, where volunteers could write what inspired them to serve. Hundreds took time to leave a note.[7]

Greg reported afterwards, "We had people from every political and religious tradition. Many have been at odds with one another. . . . But we brought them together to help people in need, and through that process, people were inspired by one another—and they learned new things." Greg was also inspired, and he learned about the Jewish tradition of *tikkun olam* (repairing the world) and of the importance of service in Islam.

Some of his fellow Christians worried that such cooperation might weaken Greg's faith by affirming the validity of other faiths. He disagreed. "When faith is just a series of ideas in your head, one does find it offensive to have it disagreed with. But when faith is lived out in action, it's more impermeable than if it's just a concept."[8] As a result of this and other efforts, participants' faith and vision grew.

Similar experiences of mutual discovery have been experienced and reported by other organizations. For example, Habitat for Humanity began as an explicitly Christian organization, with founder Millard Fuller's dream of recruiting Christians to address the widespread need for adequate housing among the poor in America and around the world. Before too long, persons of other religions joined in this cause. Interpreting his vision, Fuller began to speak of "the theology of the hammer." In a book of that title, he elaborated:

> What does "the theology of the hammer" mean? . . . Simply stated, the idea . . . is that our Christian faith . . . mandates that we do more than just talk about faith and sing about love. We must put faith and love into action to make them real, to make them come alive for people. Faith must be incarnated; that is to say, it must become more than a verbal proclamation or an intellectual assent. True faith must be acted out. . . . "The theology of the hammer" dictates that the nail be hit on the head—literally and repeatedly—until the house is built and the needy family moves in. It means, too, that continuing love and concern must be shown to the family to ensure success as a new home owner.[9]

Fuller has said that this theology motivates us to bring diverse religious communities and organizations together to work side by side "to build houses and establish viable and dynamic communities. It is acknowledging that differences of opinion exist on numerous subjects—political, philosophical, and theological—but that we can find common ground in using a hammer as an instrument to manifest God's love."[10]

This ministry is carried on with what Fuller called "biblical economics"—no profit and no interest. People pool what resources they have of money and effort to build simple, basic housing. Furthermore, each family selected for a home is expected to put in "sweat equity"— a certain number of hours of work to help construct the home. All this is done with the broad and lofty dream "to completely eliminate poverty housing and homelessness."[11]

Persons and organizations of many faith traditions have been drawn to this humanitarian work. Habitat now reports a number of interfaith projects. For example, in Atlanta, the Habitat organization and the Faith Alliance of Metro Atlanta teamed together on a project to build homes. Participants came from thirty congregations representing six different religions. These included Christian churches of various denominations, the Hindu Temple of Atlanta, Temple Sinai, and the Ismaili Muslim Center.[12] Each volunteer was to work with a partner from another congregation or faith group. As they did, mutual friendship and understanding began to grow. Volunteer Shafin Damani saw his fellow Muslim workers become more comfortable as the work progressed. He said, "I enjoyed working with these people, they're not that different than me."[13]

Another volunteer, Anuj Manocha, observed that this joint project helped him and others become more involved and connected with those outside the Hindu faith. "It's helped our congregation become more active in the community. We do a lot of work for the Hindu-based charities, but this has given us a chance to do something outside the faith. For me personally, it's been huge, because I've gotten to know other faith leaders, who I had no exposure to otherwise."[14]

Jamarcus Mayes, who was putting in the "sweat equity" working on the house where he would live, was amazed by this interfaith cooperation. "Meeting different religions, learning how they eat, how they talk, how they work with other people—like us—it's just new. New things to try. It's been fun. I didn't know all these people would come out and show love." Carolyn Mayes, his mother, added, "When [all these groups] get together, it can be a big world change for everyone."[15]

Service to others, from simple acts of kindness to vast social-action projects, have been a part of many faith traditions. In the church where I am a member, the youth group rakes leaves and trims the bushes of an older woman who is now unable to maintain her yard. A family drops by with a hot casserole for a family in which someone had a recent surgery. While such serving has been an integral part of church and other religious life, we are beginning to discover a new dimension. Joining our willingness as Christians to serve with those of other faiths can be a rich way to break down barriers, build trust, and open the door to friendship and mutual dialogue.

Mission trips are a regular part of the ministry design for middle-school and high-school youth at my church. The youth return and help the whole church share in their experience through written reflections and testimonies during worship. They have seen human tragedy, the impact of hurricanes and tornadoes, and the resilience and beauty of people living with such hardships. They have experienced the lingering pain and devastation in New Orleans, the struggle of persons with developmental disabilities in Arizona, homelessness in Washington, DC, and poverty with lack of clean water in Nicaragua. Their world grows, their willingness to explore expands, and lives of service emerge. On those journeys, they daily consider the question Pastor Kyle Gardner asks them again and again: "Where did you see God today?"

Younger children can grow through this experience of mutually shared service as well. Carol Stagner, a gifted elementary-school teacher, offers a special-emphasis summer program annually for children from our congregation and neighborhood. Last year she wanted to explore interfaith relations with the children in the program "Meet Our Neighbors," and she asked me to help. We contacted the children's leaders at the Islamic center in our area, and together we developed a plan. We would meet with the children from our church and neighborhood for the first two days, learn some basic things about the Muslim faith, and have our own service project. On the third day, children from the Islamic center would be our guests for learning activities and a service project of our choosing. On the fourth day, we would be their guests, observing and experiencing their midday prayer time and taking part in a service project of their choosing. On the fifth day, any adults and children from our group who chose to do so would worship at the noontime service at the Islamic center.

This first experience for both faith communities and their children happened almost as planned. An enthusiastic group of twelve to fifteen children, along with parents and other drivers from the Islamic center, mingled and interacted through learning games, competition, sidewalk art, and more. Children and adults brought their own lunches to fit their personal appetites and needs. The adults from the two groups seemed to enjoy visiting during lunch time, getting to know each other and sharing bites of the lunch items each had brought.

One big disappointment involved a scheduling misunderstanding for our anticipated service project. The intent was that all would ride our church bus together and provide help at Harvesters, a large agency that provides food and other supplies to more than six hundred non-profit food pantries and soup kitchens in Missouri and Kansas. When that plan fell through, our creative leader, Carol, invented an alternative. On our church grounds, we have a house that provides a place to stay for international guests or missionaries. She guided the combined group to go to the mission house to vacuum, dust, and weed, so that it would be ready for its next guests. The children were excited for something more to do, a new adventure. Although the afternoon was very hot and humid, the house was whipped into shape very quickly by children and adults working together.

The Islamic center's project was to donate new clothes to an agency called Hand to Heart, which would make them available through local schools for children from poverty-stricken families, thus providing more dignity and flexibility in the education of those children. We sat in a circle as a leader from the center guided the project. The bags of clothing the children had brought were placed in a corner. Appointed children would bring one of the bags to the center, where teenage girls neatly folded and stacked each type of clothing: blouses, shirts, sweaters, slacks, socks. When all the clothing had been brought, folded, and stacked, the girls counted and announced how many of each type of item we had brought. The children cheered as each number was announced.

Leaders and children from both congregations were enthused about the experience, the shared hospitality, and serving together. Many of us expressed the hope that this was the beginning of a continuing relationship.

Some of us will find it much easier to meet persons of other faiths by working side by side. Others may want to do something else together to further develop relationships. Whatever the reason and whatever the project, it may well be that the "theology of the hammer" will wield its power to create new and deeper community among you and your new friends.

Reflect, Discuss, Do

1. What memories did this chapter stir for you? Mission trips, a service provided for someone else, something that others did for you?

2. Does building relationships through shared service activities sound easier or harder as a way of interreligious growth? Why? In what ways?

3. What thoughts, suggestions, principles, or guidelines for shared interreligious projects did you find in this chapter? Do you have any additional ideas?

4. **Do:** Start! Perhaps do a simple project with or for a person of another religion. It can be as basic as mowing a yard, raking leaves, or bringing a meal. Contact a religious community and ask if they have a project or ministry where you can help, or invite them to participate in a shared service project.

Notes

1. Eboo Patel, *Acts of Faith: The Story of an American Muslim, the Struggle for the Soul of a Generation* (Boston: Beacon Press, 2007), xvii–xviii.

2. Eboo Patel, *Sacred Ground: Pluralism, Prejudice, and the Promise of America* (Boston: Beacon Press, 2012), 69.

3. Patel, *Acts of Faith*, 115.

4. Patel, *Sacred Ground*, 119.

5. Ibid., 70–71.

6. Much more could be said about this fascinating movement. If you'd like to know more, I recommend Patel's books, *Acts of Faith: The Story of an American Muslim, the Struggle for the Soul of a Generation*, and *Sacred Ground: Pluralism, Prejudice, and the Promise of America* and the Interfaith Youth Core web page, https://www.ifyc.org/.

7. Patel, *Sacred Ground*, 121–123.

8. David Bornstein, "A Better Way to Talk about Faith," *New York Times,* June 12, 2012, accessed September 20, 2016, http://opinionator.blogs.nytimes.com/2012/06/12/a-better-way-to-talk-about-faith/?_r=0.

9. Millard Fuller, *The Theology of the Hammer* (Macon, GA: Smyth & Helwys Publishing, Inc., 1994) 7–8.

10. Ibid.

11. Ibid.

12. Megan Frank, "Atlanta Interfaith Build," 2012, *Habitat World: The Publication of Habitat for Humanity International,* accessed September 25, 2016, http://www.habitat.org/lc/hw/archived/stories/theme-builds/interfaith/index.html.

13. Ibid.

14. Ibid.

15. Ibid.

CHAPTER NINE

The Ultimate Questions

Ask, and it will be given you; search and you will find;
knock, and the door will be opened for you.
—Matthew 7:7

The book *Undivided: A Muslim Daughter, Her Christian Mother,*
Their Path to Peace is an extended conversation between a mother
and daughter. The mother is Patricia Raybon—a devout, longtime
member of an historic African Methodist Episcopal (AME) Church in
Denver, Colorado. Her daughter is Alana Raybon, who converted to
Islam during her college years. In this book, mother and daughter address their tensions with each other about faith and religion, and they
seek reconciliation by writing about their experiences.[1] The process reveals tensions, misunderstandings, and grief over religious observances
and holidays they can no longer share as an extended family, and the
slow and cautious steps they have taken towards each other.

This is the story of a family with deep Christian roots, a family who
loves each other very much, learning to live with their new reality. It
is Christian-Muslim dialogue where it is most sensitive and the stakes
couldn't be higher. Towards the end of the book, Patricia writes about
her growing acceptance of Alana's conversion to Islam. Almost as an
aside, she adds a reflection that hit home with me. She said she'd decided to leave the salvation questions for some time in the future.[2]

That is what I have been doing up until now—postponing the "salvation question," which is actually two questions: (1) Do I believe
that the founders and followers in other religions have received

authentic revelation from God? (Again, let's think only of the three Abrahamic religions.) (2) Do I believe that persons devoted to these religions can be in right relationship with God, both here on earth and hereafter in eternity? In other words, is salvation possible within these three religions?

These aren't simple yes-or-no questions. We have only touched on this subject in previous chapters, but now we ask straight on: What do we as Christians believe regarding God's revelation and salvation in these other historic religions?

Our Christian forbears have answered these questions in a variety of ways: (1) Some said that only Christianity is true and all others are in error and in peril. Therefore, we must try to draw as many to faith in Christ as we can. (2) Others honored the search for God and peace with God in other religions, suggesting that perhaps a gracious God would not hold individuals accountable for what they did not know. (3) Still others recognized partial revelations from God in other religions but concluded that Christianity is the final and complete revelation from God. (4) Lastly, some believed that all religions are equally true—or that none of them is correct.

We now live in a shrinking and rapidly changing world. The world's major religions have grown, matured, and evolved—with more frequent and intimate contact between persons of different religions now than ever before, both in the wider world and in our religiously diverse nation. Does this constant interaction among Jews, Muslims, and Christians have any impact on what we believe about God's revelation and salvation? Should it?

This is more than an intellectual exercise. How we answer these questions changes not only the way we think—it also changes us!

Can God's Revelation Be Seen in Other Religions?

For the Abrahamic religions that we are examining, we start from a common story of call and obedience. Genesis 12:1-3 tells us, "Now the LORD said to Abram, 'Go from your country and your kindred and your father's house to the land that I will show you. I will make of you a great nation . . . and in you all the families of the earth shall be blessed.'"

That's the common biblical story of origin for each one of the three Abrahamic heritages.

The Jewish Branch of the Family Tree

What do we believe about God's revelation that led the Jewish people (the Israelites) to develop their faith narrative and practices? Do we believe that Moses had a genuine encounter and guidance from God when "the angel of the LORD appeared to him in a flame of fire out of a bush . . . the bush was blazing, yet it was not consumed" (Exodus 3:2)? Do we believe that God called Moses to deliver the children of Israel from their Egyptian slavery? Do we believe that God revealed God's self in that deliverance and the provision in the wilderness? Do we believe that God made a covenant with this people, with the Ten Commandments as the foundation of that covenant (Exodus 20:1-21)? And do we believe that God spoke through the prophets in the centuries that followed, calling the Israelites back to holiness and obedience time and time again?

For Christians, our answer is yes, God spoke through those biblical events and through the prophets who heard God's call. We affirm that God spoke through the covenant people of Israel and their heritage. Our only debate with our Jewish siblings concerns their rejection of the further revelation of God in Jesus and our affirmation of Jesus as the Incarnate Word and second person of a triune God.

As Christians, for all our ecumenical and denominational differences with one another, we know where the central foundational and guiding revelation of God is to be found for us. We resonate with the opening verse of the book of Hebrews: "Long ago God spoke to our ancestors in many and various ways by the prophets, but in these last days he has spoken to us by [a] Son" (Hebrews 1:1-2a). The birth, life, teachings, death, and resurrection of Jesus provide us the revelation of God that guides our faith and the way we live.

Nels Ferré, my theology professor in seminary, used to speak of Jesus as the "reflexive superperspective." When our eyes glazed over with confusion, he explained that the unconditional love that Jesus taught and embodied is the vantage point from which we view the history before him and after him. When we were still puzzled, Professor Ferré tried again with a simpler metaphor: "Jesus is not a ceiling; he is a skylight." In other words, we look through Jesus to God and God's revelation. This is how Jesus spoke of himself and God in the Synoptic Gospels (Matthew, Mark, and Luke). In John 14:9, Jesus said, "Whoever has seen me has seen the Father." When called good in Mark 10:18, he responded, "Why do you call me good? No one is good but God alone." If we believe these words of Jesus, what implications might our beliefs have for understanding salvation in the interfaith context?

Some fellow Christians may be uncomfortable with the view of Jesus as a skylight. I treasure it, for it honors what Jesus revealed about God, and it guides me in talking with my sisters and brothers of other faiths.

The Muslim Branch of the Family Tree

What do we believe about Islam? The first of the Five Pillars of Islam is the confession of faith, the *shahadah*: "There is no god but God, and Muhammad is the messenger of God." Do we believe this? Do we believe that Muhammad received authentic revelation? Was Muhammad a prophet like the prophets of Israel?

Swiss priest and theologian Hans Küng saw many striking parallels between Muhammad and the prophets of Israel. He noted that, like the prophets, Muhammad:

- based his work not on any office given him by the community (or its authorities) but on a special personal relationship with God.
- was a strong-willed character who saw himself as wholly penetrated by his divine vocation.
- spoke out amid a religious and social crisis . . . he stood up against the wealthy ruling class and the tradition of which it was the guardian.

• usually called himself a "warner" and wished to be nothing but God's mouthpiece and to proclaim God's word, not his own.

• tirelessly glorified the one God, who tolerates no other gods before him and who is, at the same time, the kindly Creator and merciful judge.

• insisted on unconditional obedience, devotion, and "submission" to this one God. He called for every kind of gratitude toward God and of generosity toward human beings.

• linked his monotheism to his humanism, connecting faith in the one God and God's judgment to the demand for social justice.[3]

As Küng pondered this evidence, he asked: If Judaism, Christianity, and Islam are all religions of revelation, does it not appear that the same God is speaking in the prophetic experiences of each?

Of course, just as Christianity's beliefs about Jesus as Son of God and the promised Messiah separate us theologically from Judaism, so our convictions about Jesus also become an obstacle for some Christians in relating to Muslims (and Muslims relating to Christians). As we have previously noted, the Qur'an recognizes Jesus as a great prophet—but very much a human being, not as God or as a source of salvation. Most of Jesus' first followers often saw him in a similar way—in Cleopas's words, as "Jesus of Nazareth who was a prophet mighty in deeds . . ." (Luke 24:19).

What Need Did Each Faith Originally Address?

We have been talking about the revelations received and given by historic religious figures Moses, Jesus, and Muhammad. As we explore these important questions about God's revelation and salvation as addressed by the religions that emerged from their teachings, it is helpful to ask why their messages were needed. What resulted from these lives of inspiration, witness, and sacrifice?

Moses was called to confront the oppressors of the desperate, enslaved children of Israel and to lead them to freedom as a covenant people. That covenant, often represented by the Ten Commandments, was not only vital for them as a nation but as the basis for a just and civilized world, which was to be blessed through the covenant legacy.

Jesus came to an oppressed people in their own land who were growing faint in their hopes that God would again act among them on their behalf. From Jesus' life, ministry, death, and resurrection came an empowered, witnessing, sacrificing band of followers of whom it was said, "These people have been turning the world upside down" (Acts 17:6b). Jesus' witness, presence, and guidance has been present in the founding of countless branches of Christian communities all over the globe.

Regarding Muhammad, he lived at a time and place that much needed the message he was given to share. Hans Küng summarizes this impact, noting, "They [that is, those who accepted his witness] were lifted to the heights of monotheism from the very this-worldly polytheism of the old Arabian tribal religion."[4]

This new monotheism was intimately connected to a call for justice, for concern for the rights of the weak and powerless, including the widow and the orphan, and not just the rich and powerful who were favored in the status quo he faced. This is a kindred impact to the prophets of the Hebrew Bible. From Muhammad and the message given him, the seventh-century persons on the Arabian Peninsula "received . . . a boundless supply of inspiration, courage, and strength to make a new departure in religion, toward greater truth and deeper knowledge, a breakthrough that vitalized and renewed their traditional religion."[5]

Clearly the message received and given by each of these pioneers of faith and justice had a deep and lasting impact.

The Ongoing Christian Conversation about Other Faiths

Almost three decades ago, the World Council of Churches established a program called "Dialogue with People of Living Faiths and Ideologies," which met and explored these subjects in 1990 (and have hosted consultations from time to time). As author Diana Eck, who was a participant in this WCC program, summarized, "There was profound agreement that God has found people, and people have found God, throughout human history and in the context of many religions and cultures. . . . It is in the sincere practices of their own faith that people come into relationship with God, not in spite of it."[6] She reported the consultation agreement did not go beyond that, but rather pointed to ambiguities and wrongs within the religions that prevented a clearer inclusive statement.

On the other hand, the Second Vatican Council of the Catholic Church in its "Constitution on the Church" (1965) declared clearly, "Men and women who through no fault of their own do not know the Gospel of Christ and of his Church, but who sincerely search for God and strive to do his will, as revealed by the dictates of conscience, in deeds performed under the influence on his grace, can win eternal salvation."[7]

Hans Küng pointed out that this same document embraced those who acknowledge the Creator, " . . . especially the Muslims, who profess the faith of Abraham and together with us adore the one God, the Merciful One, who will judge men on the Last Day."[8] Küng added that this has led some contemporary theologians to distinguish between "the ordinary (Christian) way of salvation and the extraordinary (non-Christian) ways of salvation."[9] Sometimes the terminology is stated as "the way" and the various "paths."

But What about John 14:6 and Acts 4:12?

Some of us may be wondering how we can even ask these questions. Did not Jesus say in John 14:6, "I am the way, and the truth, and the life. No one comes to the Father except through me"? And in Acts 4:11-12, Peter told the "rulers of the people and elders" that Jesus is "the stone that was rejected by you, the builders; it has become the cornerstone." He then proclaimed, "There is salvation in no one else, for there is no other name under heaven given among mortals by which we must be saved."

Those are significant verses that must be considered as we continue to address these questions. Let's consider each passage in its literary and historical context.

As we look at John 14:6, we recall that the Gospel of John differs rather dramatically from the other three. The Fourth Gospel is the latest of the canonical Gospels, probably written toward the end of the first century. Rather than describing specific activities and conversations that Jesus had during his ministry as the Synoptic Gospels do, John's Gospel offers a mystical reflection on the meaning of Jesus for the world. John 14 conveys a conversation in which Jesus spoke of the meaning of his death for the world. What he said was not understood by his disciples, who asked further questions. As he responded, Jesus moved even deeper into the theology of who he is and what he provides. His words "I am the way, and the truth, and the life," so seemingly simple, carry us to the depth of meaning of who he is and what he has done for us. I claim this truth wholeheartedly.

However, in the light of this context that I just described, I do not believe that Jesus intended the rest of the verse ("no one comes to the Father but by me") to be an absolute statement of exclusion for all people for all time. It is certainly true that those of us who meet Jesus as the true and living way also experience a claim on our lives to come to God through him. I also believe that the unconditional love of God, mediated by Jesus to us, has led some closer to God, even though they may not name Jesus as their Savior.

Acts 4:12, which includes Peter's statement that "there is salvation in no one else" is an exciting story of a healing, an arrest and jailing, and a court hearing. It speaks of a time of strong differences between Jews and the new followers of Jesus, who hoped the Jews would recognize Jesus as their awaited messiah and would join their cause. This did not happen to the extent that they had hoped, of course. Verse 12 stands as the climax of this story, testimony to how highly Jesus' followers esteemed him and his claim on humankind. Is it intended as an inclusion-exclusion statement for all believers of the various religions for all time? Each reader will have to decide. In the light of the context of this statement, I personally do not think so.

Exclusivism, Inclusivism, and Pluralism

As we proceed in considering the "salvation question" as it relates to interfaith relations, I will share with you the connected, but distinctive, views of two devout Christian scholars and the conclusions they have reached.

Charles Kimball, a Baptist minister and professor of comparative religions with a specialization in Islamic studies, offers an overview of the responses to this chapter's questions by noting three options for Christian theology. He describes them as exclusivism, inclusivism, and pluralism. Though there are variations in each position, they lay out the broad choices before us.

In Kimball's words, "The exclusivist position . . . rests on the unshakeable conviction that Jesus Christ provides the only valid way to salvation."[10] With no ifs, ands, or buts, believers of any other religion cannot be saved without faith in Jesus as the Son of God who died for the sins of the world.

In contrast, "the inclusivist position is distinguished by its affirmation of both the salvific presence and activity of God in all religious traditions and the full definitive revelation of God in Jesus Christ."[11] This is a dialectical position, a seeming self-contradiction saying both yes and no to other traditions. This view suggests that revelation and salvation can be found in other religions, but the most foundational truths about God and salvation are found in the Christian faith.

The pluralist position, Kimball suggests, offers a third option. "Advocates of pluralistic theologies of religion see Christianity neither as the only means to salvation nor as the fulfillment of other religious traditions. Rather the pluralist position affirms the viability of various paths."[12]

About twenty years after Kimball delineated these three options, another scholar, Paul Knitter, wrote *Introducing Theologies of Religion*, in which he considers not three but four different theological understandings of the various religions. Some of these have a resemblance to the categories Kimball described.[13] These four are:

• **The Replacement Model,** in which the basic view is of "Only One True Religion" (similar to Kimball's "exclusivist" view). In this model, the only true revelation and the only true salvation are in the religion one holds. From a Christian perspective, then, only Christianity provides salvation, meaning that persons of another religion may experience salvation only by *replacing* their current religious faith with faith in Jesus.

• **The Fulfillment Model** might be summarized as "The One Fulfills the Many" (similar to Kimball's "inclusivist" position). In this view, an individual embraces ultimate truth in his or her own religion (which is the ultimate *fulfillment* of belief), but, at the same time, is able to dialogue appreciatively with others.

• **The Mutuality Model** suggests there are "Many True Religions Called to Dialogue." Those in this school of thought discover *mutuality* through both mystical and prophetic bridges. They advocate acting together, both in prayer and worship and in prophetic and caring actions in the world, and then talking about what they hold in common.

• **The Acceptance Model** viewpoint may be summarized as "Many True Religions: So Be It." This postmodern view *accepts* the existence of multiple faith narratives, each with meaning and significance for those who embrace it.[14] (Kimball's pluralist type has some resemblance to each of these last two.)

Knitter also considers the place of Jesus in each of these models. Individuals who choose the Replacement model ask adherents of the other models, "Is it not possible that Jesus of Nazareth constitutes something thoroughly surprising, thoroughly exceptional and unique in the history of humanity?"[15] Replacement adherents answer yes to their own question and conclude that further conversations must include recognition of Jesus' unique role in revealing God's grace and bridging the gap between God and fallen humanity.

Those affirming any of the other models attempt to balance two basic and vital truths: the universality of God's love and the particularity and uniqueness of Jesus. To help us understand this, Knitter notes the contrast between *Jesus as savior* and *Jesus as sacrament*. The view of "Jesus as savior" is to see him as the one who fixes what is broken, or, to change the image, who builds the bridge to connect us to God. The view of "Jesus as sacrament" is that he is "the one who reveals what is already given but not yet evident." In this view Jesus "make[s] real that which is already there, but which we cannot see or feel without the sacrament's [Jesus'] power to reveal it."[16]

This may seem to be tortured language, hard to follow. But what Knitter is saying merits careful consideration. He is suggesting that when we realize we are deeply loved and cared for by God as revealed in Jesus, we are given eyes to see God's presence in the spiritual journeys of people in other religions as well. This is akin to the metaphor I mentioned earlier from my professor Nels Ferré, that Jesus is a skylight—through him we see the majesty and love of the heavens that shines on us, all of us.

These writers have been helpful to me as I try to think through where I stand on these questions. At this point in my religious pilgrimage, I find myself agreeing with the second of Kimball's three possibilities; I am an inclusivist. I agree with the second of Knitter's models, the Fulfillment Model. I treasure my journey and membership within the Christian community, and I treasure the rich biblical literature grounded in the love of God experienced through Jesus. I also believe that the prophets of these other religions received authentic revelation from God and that persons can be in right relationship with God within those religions.

One other factor contributes to my conclusion—probably the most powerful and important one: my experience with persons of these other religions. I have met people who give themselves generously to an honest, deep rapport across traditional religious lines. As I sense the goodness of these persons, as I see them actively contributing to the healing of our community, and as I worship as a guest in their places of worship, I have a clear sense that I am in the presence of

God and of God's saints, whatever their religion.

This is where my journey has brought me thus far. In the next chapter, we'll look at trying to be Christlike with other populations who do not have specific religious beliefs or affiliations. Then we'll talk about being Christlike in navigating the differences Christians have with one another. Perhaps this includes some differences you may have with me!

Reflect, Discuss, Do

1. What questions, if any, has this chapter answered for you? What questions, if any, has it raised?

2. When you ask yourself the "salvation questions" in this chapter—about the possibility of God's revelation and right relationship with God in other religions—what is clear to you? What are you still exploring?

3. What person of another religion—either a public figure or someone you know—seems to you to be close to God and represents God's love and justice?

4. **Do:** Write your credo, or your questions, about these subjects. Find an accepting person who will listen as you read it aloud. Invite that person's response.

Notes

1. Patricia Raybon and Alana Raybon. *Undivided: A Muslim Daughter, Her Christian Mother, Their Path to Peace* (Nashville: W, Publishing Group of Thomas Nelson, 2015).

2. Ibid., 225–228.

3. Küng, Hans, Josef van Ess, Heinrich von Stietencron, and Heinz Bechert. Translated by Peter Heinegg. *Christianity & World Religions: Paths to Dialogue* (Maryknoll: Orbis Books, 1997), 25–26.

4. Ibid., 27.

5. Ibid.

6. Diana Eck, "On Seeking and Finding in the World's Religions," The Christian Century, May 2, 1990, 455, as quoted in Charles

Kimball, *Striving Together: A Way Forward in Christian-Muslim Relations* (Maryknoll, NY: Orbis Books, 1991), 96.

7. Pope Paul VI, *Gaudium Et Spes* (Pastoral Constitution on the Church in the Modern World), Article 16, Second Vatican Council, December 7, 1965, accessed October 20, 2016, http://www.vatican.va /archive/hist_councils/ii_vatican_council/documents/vat-ii_cons_19651207_gaudium-et-spes_en.html.

8. Küng, *Christianity & World Religions*, 23.

9. Ibid., 24.

10. Kimball, *Striving Together*, 71.

11. Ibid., 72.

12. Ibid., 78.

13. Paul F. Knitter, *Introducing Theologies of Religion* (Maryknoll, NY: Orbis Books, 2002).

14. Ibid., vii–ix.

15. Ibid., 53.

16. Ibid., 105.

CHAPTER TEN

A Christlike Presence among the "Nones"

When [Jesus] saw the crowds, he had compassion for them, because they were harassed and helpless, like sheep without a shepherd.—Matthew 9:36

"A profound spiritual change is going on in America. No matter how organized religions try to ignore, challenge, adapt, or protest it, our society is being deeply changed by [this pervasive ethos] . . . ."—Linda A. Mercadante[1]

Our focus now changes from our relationships with persons in the Abrahamic religions to another aspect of the changed and changing North American religious scene. I refer to the rise of the spiritual but not religious persons (SBNRs). Sometimes they are called the "Nones," as that is what they check as their religious affiliation on questionnaires. Others use the word "Dones" when referring to individuals who have withdrawn from their churches and now hold a wide variety of beliefs.

This is a painful topic for me personally. I have devoted my life to promoting the compassionate and redemptive message of the Christian faith. It saddens me when I see once-strong congregations shrink to a shadow of what they were. Many have become too small to afford a full-time pastor. There is also declining enrollment in seminaries and diminished opportunities for their graduates. (Perhaps I need a chapter on this subject even more than you do!) Clearly we need some perspective on this important subject.

A Sociological-Historical Perspective

Scholars Robert Putnam and David Campbell offer historical and sociological insights on the growth of this movement. They note that the 1950s marked the high point of civil religion in the United States— that is, public affirmation and encouragement of religious practice.[2] (That was the decade when I studied for ministry and began my pastorates.) The anxieties of World War II seemed to have revived religious interest (which had lagged some in the 1920s and 1930s), and churches were booming again.

Then, in the next half-century we experienced a huge "shock and two aftershocks." The shock, Putnam and Campbell said, came in the 1960s, with a number of sudden and drastic changes in youth culture and the way the next generation tended to view religion. They categorize this shock as "sex, drugs, rock-and-roll, and 'God is dead.'"[3] The 1960s was a "perfect storm" for US institutions, whether political, social, sexual, or religious. This was the decade of the unpopular and violent Vietnam War, as well as the assassinations of John and Robert Kennedy, Martin Luther King Jr., and Malcolm X—with all the upheaval and reverses in politics and civil rights that came with those murders.

Along with these events and changes in culture came the huge babyboomer population, with a larger portion of young adults entering colleges than ever before. The introduction of the birth-control pill was associated with a vast number of rapid changes in sexual mores and practices. The use of pot and LSD was growing on college campuses, which were also energized to the point of exploding with the ongoing civil rights movement, the antiwar movement, and other movements for civil rights and equal protections under the law. This was a time when old forms, including church life and historic Judeo-Christian beliefs, were widely questioned and increasingly abandoned.

Trying to make sense of what was happening, theologians reflected on and wrote about the radical changes in belief and practice. Some used the metaphor of the "death of God," and the public was affected. Sales of books on religious topics dropped by one-third during this time. In addition, the Second Vatican Council brought ferment and change to Roman Catholic churches and others of the Christian faith.

That was the shock.

The first aftershock, Putnam and Campbell suggest, was the rise of religious conservatism.[4] As part of the reaction to the sudden, varied, and bewildering changes of the sixties, seventies, and eighties, a marked growth of membership and participation in conservative (evangelical) churches occurred, including the rise of nondenominational congregations. Televangelist Jerry Falwell and former Southern Baptist pastor turned media mogul and *700 Club* host Pat Robertson became widely influential in both religion and politics in the eyes of the media.

This trend in turn led to a second aftershock. In the 1990s and 2000s, this aftershock was "youth disaffection from religion."[5] From the 1990s on, more and more people were not happy with the large public presence of conservative Christians, particularly their influence in ideological causes and support of political candidates. This disaffection was felt throughout the US population, but it was strongest among young adults under the age of thirty. Putnam and Campbell concluded that this initial shock and two aftershocks, and all of their ramifications, account in large part for the growth of the Nones.[6]

There have always been some Nones in America who have no religious affiliation, but their numbers have grown vastly since the 1960s. According to the General Social Survey, the Nones were 5 percent of the population in 1972, 7 percent in 1975, and 8 percent in 1990, and the numbers increased dramatically to 14 percent in 2000, 18 percent in 2010, and at least 20 percent in 2012.[7] The rise to 22.8 percent in 2015 represents more Nones than mainline Protestants (the broad religious group where I place myself) and also more than Roman Catholics. In 2017, one fifth of the US population consider themselves to be Nones, or nearly fifty million people, with one third of them under thirty years old.

If we look at religion in North America from a wider sweep of history than the last sixty to seventy years, we see an even broader religious range of movement. From early on, many persons (but not all) came to the United States to escape religious oppression in their lands of origin. They came seeking freedom to believe and worship as they saw fit—or not.

As the centuries have passed, these historic American heritages have come to another stage. We are in a new age where, unlike our forebears, we "do not inherit religious identity as a given, a matter of kin and tribe."[8] Not only the Nones, but all of us, are called to make our spiritual choices, form or reform our religious communities, dream dreams, and offer challenges adequate for the age in which we live.

What do we see as we consider these Nones? Krista Tippett, a theologically educated journalist and host of the National Public Radio show *On Being*, sees hope in this situation:

> The growing universe of the Nones—the new nonreligious—is one of the most spiritually vibrant and provocative places in modern life. It is not a world in which spiritual life is absent. It is a world that resists religious excesses and shallows. Large swaths of this universe are wild with ethical passion and open to theological curiosity. They are expressing this in unexpected places and unexpected ways.[9]

To support this claim, she reflects on two of her interviewees. One is Nathan Schneider, a millennial intellectual with contributions in journalism, academics, social activities, and religion. After exploring religion through his adolescence, he chose to be baptized Roman Catholic at age eighteen, drawn both by the medieval contemplative tradition and the courageous social witness of Dorothy Day. He has written creatively about the Occupy Wall Street movement and of its involvement, in the wake of Hurricane Sandy, to form Occupy Sandy. This young-adult movement gathered supplies for the needy and took them to churches in the affected areas. They called upon the churches to be the church and distribute these supplies to those hurricane victims who needed them.[10]

Her other example is Gen Xer Shane Claiborne. In introducing him, she says that among the young Nones are "people who haven't rejected the faith of their childhood, but grew up allergic to stridency and determined to reform it."[11] Shane was born in Tennessee and spent teenage years canvassing for vice-presidential candidate Dan Quayle. He then attended the historically Baptist college, Eastern (now Palmer) University, outside of Philadelphia, drawn by its commitment to social justice. Afterwards, he and some friends became involved with a large number of homeless people who had moved into an abandoned church in Philadelphia and were facing forced removal. In time, Shane and a growing number of like-minded friends moved in with them and formed an intentional community, now known as "The Simple Way." This radical Christian community worships together, cares for one another, and responds to the needs of the community, neighborhood, and city. Shane's journey has also taken him to serve with the Sisters of Mercy in Calcutta and learn from Mother Teresa, as The Simple Way community tries to build a better world following the teachings of Jesus.

Near the end of his conversation with Tippett, Claiborne commented:

> I'm convinced that if the Christian church loses this generation, it will not be because we didn't entertain them, but because we didn't dare them with the truth of the world. It won't be because we'd made the gospel too hard but because we made it too easy, and we just played games with kids and didn't actually challenge them to think about how they live.[12]

Tippett concludes that "the Nones of this age are ecumenical, humanist, trans-religious. But in their midst are analogs to the original monastics: spiritual rebels and seekers on the margins of established religion, pointing tradition back to its own untamable, countercultural, service-oriented heart."[13]

Now that is a different perspective than the sadness with which I began this chapter! I deeply appreciate Tippett's point of view and the examples she discovered. On her NPR program, she finds creative people who explore the fringes and depths of belief. Hers is a focused perspective that upholds a viewpoint that stands in contrast to what others may see.

Tippett's examples are of deeply spiritual people who do not fit the conventional mold. It will also be helpful for us to take a broader look at this vast and growing population of spiritual but not religious people.

A Sensitive Investigation of SBNRs

Professor and author Linda Mercadante offers us this broad investigation of "spiritual but not religious" (SBNR) individuals. A former SBNR herself, the child of Catholic and Jewish parents, and a long-time searcher through many religious paths, she became a Presbyterian clergy and professor of historical theology. She notes that she found the church and faith she was looking for at about the time when this part of the Christian church seemed to be falling apart.[14]

While much has been reported about this growing trend of SBNRs in the North American religious scene, little investigation has been conducted regarding some very important questions, such as who are these SBNR people, what do they believe, and why are their numbers increasing so significantly?

Mercadante set out to gain insight into those questions. She interviewed nearly a hundred SBNRs, in one- to two-hour recorded sessions that were then transcribed and analyzed. She began by asking her interviewees to describe their spiritual journeys, and then inquired about their beliefs on four major topics: transcendence, human nature, community, and afterlife.[15]

She found persons to interview from each of the adult life stage cohorts from the Greatest Generation (born from about 1901–1924) to the Millennials (born from about 1981–2002). Her smallest group of interviewees were Millennials, even though the proportion of Millennials who are SBNR is the largest among US adults. About one-third of Millennials see themselves as SBNR.[16]

What drew persons into this way of thinking, and how do they see themselves? Mercadante received a number of different responses and much variation within each. She summarized these responses into five broad categories. "Dissenters" are persons who stayed away from institutional religion and were suspicious of it. They may have been hurt, either personally or theologically, by it. "Casuals" see spiritual practices as mainly functional. Spirituality does not have their full attention, nor is it their organizing principle for living.[17] "Explorers" are those who try one thing after another, moving on to yet other possibilities. They have a wanderlust and fascination for the novel spiritual options. "Seekers" are those actually looking for a spiritual home. They may be hoping to reclaim an earlier spiritual identity, or something slightly different, or perhaps a new religion altogether. "Immigrants" are those who have moved to a new spiritual place and are in the process of adjusting to a new community and a new identity.[18]

As I read these descriptions, I find myself remembering Joan—a bright, inquisitive wife and mother in her mid-thirties. Joan contacted me because she heard a comment about the church where I served as pastor from a friend at her bridge club. This led to a series of stimulating conversations over the next several weeks. She had been a member of other churches, left them, and wondered if perhaps our congregation was her spiritual destination. She asked good questions about our beliefs, heritage, and practices, and she pushed hard when my answers were unclear or unsatisfying.

In time, she started participating in our church life, along with her husband and children. I was happy that I had seemed to help a seeker find her spiritual home where she could worship, grow, and serve. But after a few years, Joan and her family's participation became more sporadic. I learned that Joan was fascinated by the Jehovah's Witness callers that had knocked on her door. I lost contact with her, but a mutual friend told me that Joan's interest in the Jehovah's Witnesses had faded, and she was again looking around. I had assumed she was a "seeker" on her way to becoming an "immigrant" (in Mercadante's terms), but perhaps she was more of an "explorer."

Common Themes among "Nones"

Mercadante identified some common themes that were expressed by these SBNRs across this spectrum of age and experience. One theme was an opposition to and criticism of Western religious concepts. Their choices might be described as "post-Christian spirituality . . . spirituality standing on its own two feet and broken from the moorings of Christian tradition."[19] Many perceived the religions they left as having exclusive, all-or-nothing attitudes, which they rejected. They refused to accept the idea of having a traditional authority over one's life. Instead, they welcomed the opportunity to make their own personal choice about spirituality. In other words, the locus of authority moved from an exterior source to within the person.

Many SBNRs expressed disappointment that some religionists' ethical behavior did not measure up to their stated beliefs. Coupled with this was a widespread view that all religions are essentially the same, that mystical encounters from one faith to another are similar, and that no religion gets it exactly right.

SBNRs often demonstrate widespread enthusiasm for combining elements from various new trends and old spiritual traditions. Many turned to nature as a source of spiritual experience and renewal. They might view this as their sole spirituality or in conjunction with other practices.[20]

Mercadante's findings suggest a multitude of beliefs and practices among SBNRs. SBNRs include persons who are still involved in their churches, even as staff members, and others who are students in theological schools. Social scientists have discerned that today's boundaries between the religious and the SBNR are quite vague and porous. They note, for example, that in response to different surveys, some persons—nominal church members, for example—might state a church preference, and other times say they have none, without changing their behavior in any way.

Who Are the "Dones"?

What about the "Dones"?—those who may have had long and deep involvement in the life of their church, but do so no longer. Although books have been written about these people,[21] I will speak of those I know since I live among them every day and hear some of their stories. Here are a few representative examples.

A man who was a Sunday school teacher for adult classes and active in his Methodist church had a strong disagreement with his pastor, who had a more liberal view of Jesus than he did. Rather than work through it with that pastor or find another church, he withdrew and invested himself more deeply in his "sandwich generation" responsibilities of parenting, grandparenting, and caring for his mother afflicted with Alzheimer's. He has not been back to church.

I know numerous married couples who have very different religious backgrounds, beliefs, and desires. Their differences and conflicts over this may stymie active participation in a religious community or denomination. I remember a couple whose religious difference was not large—she was Baptist and he was Methodist. But rather than offending either set of parents, they stayed away from church for years. In my opinion, all too often, rather than work at the uncomfortable task of sorting this out and making decisions or compromises, such couples avoid the subject—and participating in a local faith community—perhaps for years, and even for life.

Several of my young adult friends had profound faith experiences as children and youths at retreats and on mission trips. This inspired a high idealism of service and they have entered professions to carry on that vision. They advocate for the underprivileged, promote immigration, teach in inner-city schools, offer counsel and support to the troubled or dying, or work in the medical healing field. Their important work, along with family demands and leisure opportunities, fill their lives. They live their lives of service outside of the faith community that stimulated their calling. I recently visited with two persons, adults who had been in my youth groups and Christian education years ago. They both said that was an important time, and they hoped for the same thing for their children—but, apparently, not for themselves.

One middle-aged woman did what the church asked of her for years: served and chaired many boards and committees. In time, she grew frustrated with her church's bureaucratic structure and despaired of accomplishing anything to strengthen the children's ministries that she loved. She resigned from the boards, withdrew from the church, and volunteered at her local children's hospital instead.

These experiences usually happened much more slowly than the stories seem to portray—perhaps over years. Still, they are part of the picture I am exploring with you in this chapter.

While spiritual beliefs among the Nones and Dones vary, some have abandoned belief in any kind of deity. And so, a small percentage of these disenchanted groups are atheist, often estimated at 2 percent of the US population, but perhaps larger in light of the attention given to the group called the "new atheists." Christopher Hitchens and Richard Dawkins, among others, are leaders in this movement. This point of view is perhaps best summarized by the magazine cover story, "The New Atheism: No Heaven, No Hell, Just Science."[22] These new atheists may still include themselves in the SBNR category, but their spirituality is not connected to a deity or religious institution or tradition.

Recently I became aware of a new organization in my city called "Oasis." Their website announces: "Oasis is a place for the non-religious to come together to celebrate the human experience." They list their core values as these: "People are more important than beliefs. . . . Reality is known through reason. . . . Human hands solve human problems. . . . Meaning comes from making a difference. . . . Be accepting and be accepted."[23]

I visited one of their weekly Sunday morning assemblies, where at least a couple hundred people gathered. There was much sociability, coffee and doughnuts, a performing musical group, and a presentation on the importance of classical languages by a local professor and a member of their community. I was welcomed and engaged in conversation in this high-energy gathering.

According to their website, "Oasis Communities include people who identify as Agnostic, Humanist, Freethinker, Atheist, Skeptic, Deists, and even progressive Theists of various types." The site also mentions that the first Oasis community was in Houston and that Oasis communities are being formed in other cities.[24] While some attendees are weary of church life, others whose beliefs have changed seem drawn to a community that supports them in their SBNR journey.

How Can We Be Christlike toward SBNRs?

The SBNRs whom Mercadante interviewed give us some clues for how to respond in a caring way. For one, she discovered some prevailing but wrong understandings about the religions they were rejecting. A significant percentage of those interviewed believed that traditional religion practitioners were exclusivist and unable to see beyond their own boundaries. Though this generalization is not true of all people of faith, SBNRs held the stereotype strongly and felt that therefore their belief in universal truth was on a higher spiritual plain. SBNRs also were convinced that, concerning the afterlife, churchgoers held a strong "my way or the highway" point of view, that only those in one's own faith community would be accepted by God. Again, surveys reveal how mistaken this view is, but it is a strongly held belief among SBNRs.[25]

Mercadante noted a good amount of religious illiteracy. Persons who left a church did not know that church's teachings, contributions, or heritage, nor did many who remained. They also demonstrated a dearth of deep theological reasoning and thinking. If theology is indeed, as the classic definition says, "faith seeking understanding," and if it can offer ways to reflect on experience, beliefs, and thought, then theology is a valuable gift. We all have questions greater than ourselves, questions about the purpose of life, and of one's own life, questions about hope, about suffering, about death. Mercadante reflects, "Many interviewees were grappling with just these sorts of questions. Most, however, had not been given tools adequate for the task."[26] When the teachings of one's heritage are resisted, one's childhood catechism rejected, a new path of discovery is needed. Many were ignorant of knowledge of any permanent theological thought world, and thus these persons were wrestling with huge existential questions with meager resources.

So what is a Christlike response to SBNRs who face such dilemmas? Clearly the Christian is called to take spiritual formation and Christian education about one's roots, heritage, and beliefs with utter seriousness. And the church is commissioned to offer this education and encourage participation. When confronted with such gaps or misunderstandings, it is important to be ready to share more accurate and deeply held interpretations. And it is important to do this respectfully, calmly, and with the authority of a first-hand faith, faithfully explored and deeply held.

But Mercadante does not stop there. She also points out that this rapidly growing movement has gifts to offer those of us who are not participants. She suggests that SBNRs may help us see our blind spots. Perhaps their humanizing of God, emphasis on personal growth, human self-determination, and focus on the natural world can propel us to reexamine and restate our beliefs for a new and changing world.[27] SBNRs may also lead the rest of us into discovering the benefits of multiple religious participation. This might be on a subconscious level, simply adopting practices (such as yoga, for example) from another religion. Or it might be more extensive, embracing key concepts from two or more religions. We will speak more of this in the closing chapter.

Further, NPR's Krista Tippett's exhilaration at the excitement that some of these young adult pioneers are bringing to the world nudges of all of us. We are called to listen, respond, and join their cause of changing the way we have been doing things, quite probably for far too long.

Before concluding this chapter, let's consider one more aspect of the challenge of living in this world with a multitude of beliefs. Recently, a couple wrote to ask advice of a newspaper columnist. Their dilemma was how to deal with the parents of their elementary-school daughter's best friend. When the two families met, the friend's parents spoke enthusiastically about their church and invited this couple to attend. They responded that they were not believers and did not participate in religion. The couple thought that would be the end of it, but since then the invitations to church activities have come more and more frequently. The nonbelieving couple feels their clearly stated position is being disrespected. "What should we do?" they asked the advice columnist.

More to our purpose, what should the churchgoing parents do? Clearly, the invitations are given out of the best of intentions, and clearly, at least as indicated by the letter to the newspaper, the invitations were experienced as offensive. How should the believing couple be Christlike in regard to these persons with whom their daughter will associate during times the friends are together? I've shared a number of my opinions in this chapter. I'll leave this one to you.

I close with Mercadante's challenging and hopeful conclusion:

> It is important that Christians face forward into the theological and spiritual headwind of this burgeoning movement. If they do so, they may well repeat the feats of previous generations who overcame other seemingly impossible crises for the church. . . . Today's Christians, like their ancestors, can reframe the gospel in ways that again speak to the deepest human longings and needs. They can create alternative faith communities which give persons a supportive context in which to live this out. And they can develop new ways to cooperate with God's healing work in the world.[28]

Reflect, Discuss, Do

1. What did you learn about Nones, Dones, and new atheists that you didn't know before?

2. In this chapter I have summarized three opinions about the SBNRs and persons of kindred views: Trippett's enthusiasm at their ferment and creativity, Mercadante's empathic and sympathetic

description, and my sadness. Which mood best matches yours? What is your calling in relation to Nones, Dones, and new atheists?

3. If you were the churchgoing parent described above, how would you relate in a Christlike way with the nonbelieving, non-practicing parents of your child's friend?

4. Where do you need to grow in understanding your faith community's heritage and beliefs and your thinking about the perspective of faith on life's dilemmas and disappointments?

5. **Do:** Have a listening, nonjudgmental visit with a None, Done, or new atheist. Don't argue. Listen to learn.

Notes

1. Linda A. Mercadante, *Belief without Borders: Inside the Minds of the Spiritual but Not Religious* (New York: Oxford University Press, 2014), xvi.

2. Robert D. Putnam and David E. Campbell, *American Grace: How Religion Divides and Unites Us* (New York: Simon and Schuster, 2010), 91–133.

3. Ibid., 91.

4. Ibid., 100–120.

5. Ibid., 120.

6. Ibid., 132–133.

7. Mercadante, *Belief without Borders,* 2.

8. Krista Tippett, *Becoming Wise: An Inquiry into the Mystery and Art of Living* (New York: Penguin Press, 2016), 170.

9. Ibid., 171.

10. Ibid.

11. Ibid., 175.

12. Ibid., 178–179.

13. Ibid.

14. Mercadante, *Belief without Borders,* xiii.

15. Ibid., 15.

16. Ibid., 36–50.

17. Ibid., 51–58.

18. Ibid., 58–67.

19. Ibid., 71.

20. Ibid., 88–91.

21. *Church Refugees: Sociologists reveal why people are DONE with church but not their faith* (Loveland, CO, Group Publishing: 2015) by Josh Packard and Ashleigh Hope is one such book. You might also want to read *You Lost Me: Why Young Christians Are Leaving the Church . . . and Rethinking Faith* by David Kinnaman and Aly Hawkins (Grand Rapids: Baker Books, 2016).

22. Greg M. Epstein, *Good without God: What a Billion Nonreligious People Do Believe* (New York: William Morrow, 2009), xvi.

23. Kansas City Oasis website, 2015, accessed October 15, 2016, http://www.kcoasis.org/.

24. Ibid.

25. Mercadante, *Belief without Borders*, 202.

26. Ibid., 228.

27. Ibid., 255.

28. Ibid., 258.

CHAPTER ELEVEN

Shared Life with Fellow Christians Who Disagree with Me

I ask . . . on behalf of those who will believe in me through their word, that they may all be one. As you, Father, are in me and I in you, may they also be in us, so that the world may believe that you have sent me. —John 17:20-21

It is strange but true: often we are closer to persons who are not part of our own family than we are to the family into which we were born. A neighbor, classmate, teammate, or roommate, for example, may be such a person to whom we are drawn. As one gets to know the other, sharing dreams, secrets, hopes, and regrets, and all, a deep bond develops. People use phrases such as "brothers from another mother" or "sisters from another mister" to describe this closeness that many experience beyond their familial bonds.

This is true of Christian denominations and of the wider Christian community as well. Our heritage and membership may be within a particular Christian tradition. But a wide variety of beliefs, interests, and priorities exist within that denomination; some we share, and some we don't. These topics may sometimes be contentious, making participation within our own traditions feel uneasy, tense, and unsatisfying. It may be more gratifying to find Christians in other traditions or faith groups with whom we feel at home. We can experience these tensions with an individual, our home congregation, or our denomination.

Our conflicts with one another as Christians may begin with how we view our Scriptures. This is despite the fact that we have much in common with how we engage our Bibles. Most Christians believe that the Bible is a means by which we encounter God; it is a book of the acts of God. We look to the Bible for ethical guidance, and its teachings reveal how we as God's people are to live. We believe that God renews God's people through the Bible. Furthermore, we believe, as John Robinson told pilgrims leaving for the "new world," that God has more light and truth yet to break forth out of God's Holy Word.

With all that we hold in common about Scripture, we also have some differences in how we interpret Scripture. Over the last century, scholars have studied the cultures in which the Bible was written, its literary forms, the biblical languages, the canonization of Scripture, as well as its transmission. All these discoveries have implications for how we view and interpret the Bible, which in turn impacts our differences with one another. We may disagree on which topics the Bible is authoritative. Some of us say the Bible is authoritative in all matters: faith, practice, science, history, geography, psychology, marriage, and human relationships among others. Others of us differentiate some biblical teachings as having broad authority while others apply to the particular culture and age in which they were written.

This leads to another difference: how to interpret the cultural and social settings in the Bible, and what Bible passages say in response to those settings and in that context. It has been suggested that we need to distinguish between what was written for an age and what was written for all ages. Of course, that is difficult to discern and we may be wrong—either way!

Ethicist Dennis Hollinger has sorted out what we have been describing and comes to this conclusion: "The inspiration of Scripture was not a dictation from heaven but embodied both divine and human elements. Nonetheless, God was providentially at work in both the revelatory events and the spoken or written word in such a way that what we have is what God intended."[1]

Hollinger's is a defensible and substantial conclusion. Others, however, have a different view of Scripture. They have noted that the word *inspired* comes closer to the root meaning of the word for *breath*. "The Bible is in-breathed with God's spirit. God is found there. God is met there. God guides there. God renews and invites there. God inspires there. But for those of us who read this way, inspiration is a more mysterious, indirect process than the former group finds, less likely to provide clear guidance and directives."[2]

Further, the Bible describes God as speaking through history—both the history of individuals and the history of the ages. Does this imply that God continues to reveal God's self and guidance in history today—in both our personal histories (life stories) and the history of the world through today? I believe the answer to that is yes. You will have to decide what you believe about God's continuing revelation and guidance.

In addition to differences in how we view Scripture, Christians also have differences in what we believe, what we emphasize, and what our faith priorities are. We also differ in what practices (such as Lord's Supper and Baptism) we engage, how and when we engage them, and who is allowed to experience these observances with us. We also hold some radically different views on issues of family, gender, and sexuality. Throughout the centuries, and perhaps now more than ever, we have disagreed about celibacy, polygamy, divorce, remarriage, abortion, sexual orientation, gender identity, and same-sex marriages. Some of these disagreements are deep and strong, and at times have even become violent. These differences of opinion and biblical interpretation have led to a divided Christianity—and we are the ones for whom Jesus prayed that we be one as Jesus and the Father are one so that the world may know that God sent Jesus (see John 17:22)!

I have stated this division starkly. But of course, there is also another side. In seeking that oneness, Christians have reached out to each other across our many differences. It happens on a one-to-one basis. I have friends who disagree with me on many vital beliefs and practices, some of them my former students. These are relationships I value as rich and meaningful, and I need these friendships. I experience these persons as kind and caring, good persons believing and living out their faith in their Christian walk, as I am doing out of mine. My thinking is sharpened, and my perspective on those who disagree with me is softened by these relationships. We keep each other honest.

Clergy associations and councils of churches also sometimes achieve greater accord across their many differences. I was pleased to read the description of such growth in one ministerial association in Richland County, Wisconsin. *The Christian Century* magazine offered two stories, a little over two years apart, about this association and its transformation. The story began in 2009, when this Richland County Ministerial Association was in serious decline. Very few pastors were attending any longer, and only one was a conservative evangelical. That was Michael Breininger, who said he came not to support the group but to silence it. He recalled, "I was deeply concerned that the differences between the theological liberals and conservatives, and the ranting of those wanting everyone else to adopt their agenda, were a disgrace to the name of Christ."[3] Then, much to his chagrin, he was elected president. Though initially stunned, he knew deep inside that the Spirit of God was nudging him to be a builder, but that he would need "a heart change and a new vision." So he set about to help the association revive. He insisted that topics be discussed at the RCMA meetings in a respectful and timely fashion. He drafted a paper called "Pastoral Courtesies," which included ten rules of civil conversation that the association accepted as he tried to build expectations.

His efforts impressed Larry Engel, a liberal Lutheran pastor, who was increasingly, by his own description, a "lonely liberal." Mike's leadership of the association had a ring of truth. "I liked that a lot," Engel said. "He was a leader and a disciple, one who had integrity, humility, and a deep commitment to the gospel. I was beginning to feel less lonely and part of something purposeful, challenging, and Christlike."[4] And so he went up and complimented Michael on his leading a productive meeting. Breininger recalls, "I was surprised by the compliment.

I don't recall a liberal pastor ever complimenting me about anything. Maybe the liberals were more than just red-faced name callers who thought they needed to inform the evangelicals of their foolish antiquated views of the Bible."[5]

That conversation was the beginning of a friendship between the two that developed slowly and cautiously. Gradually, each discovered he could share beliefs and viewpoints, argue vigorously for them, disagree just as vigorously, and not lose their friendship. They also discovered a wide number of community needs to which the clergy association, along with other area leaders, could respond. As trust and strength grew, the churches represented in the clergy association worshipped together more frequently. They also cooperated in identified ministry needs, which included housing centers for the homeless and education programs to bring together area industries that needed employees with high-school seniors who too frequently abandoned the county soon after graduation.

When Michael's two-year term as president of the association ended, he nominated Larry to succeed him, so that the vigor of the shared ministries might continue and grow. Larry Engel concludes this remarkable story with these words:

> Discussing, praying, and worshiping together several times a year with Richland County Ministerial Association members builds trust and understanding. Engaging with public leaders in projects that change the culture is kingdom building. Our ministerial association may be small, but we are strong because we work with a broad base of regional leaders. More and more of us are no longer strangers.[6]

Members are now able to strongly disagree with each other about such topics as same-sex marriages without tearing themselves apart.

I offer this story to provide background and perspective for exploring our differences on the topic of this book. I hope that as fellow Christians we can build a similar level of trust, respect, dialogue, and support as we work on our differences with each other on how to be Christlike with persons of other religions in this interreligious world.

As we earlier noted, there are at least two distinct positions that Christians may hold. Charles Kimball called the one the "exclusivist" position and the other "inclusivist." Though these are rather awkward terms, at least they are not pejorative of either stance, so we will go with them. Here are a few of the places in my exploration so far where my inclusivist view may differ from yours:

• When I considered the question of what we intend—conversation or conversion—recognizing that the motivations for conversation and conversion are closer than I earlier realized, I opted for conversation as my primary objective.

• When I recognized that there was much more to explore in the interfaith discussions than I had explored previously, I was blessed by the rich gifts of hospitality, generosity, and deep spirituality in the persons I encountered. I also realized that other Christians might believe that, as pleasant as this was, it would be more faithful to see these conversations as steps to hoped-for conversions.

• When I asked myself whether I believe that God's revelation occurred in the founding and development of each of the Abrahamic religions, my answer was yes. I believe God spoke to and through Abraham, Moses, Jesus, and Muhammad, calling into being new and healing movements.

• And when I asked myself whether I believe that persons in these religions can be in right relationship with God, here and hereafter— if they could experience salvation—again I answered yes.

My hunch is that some—perhaps many—Christians of goodwill may not want to go with me in these convictions. That is quite understandable. Much of my life, I did not either. I am surprised and still growing—perhaps groping—to find my way. Critiques of my views can come from both sides. Some may see me as heretical, and others may see me as too timid in this "postmodern" age. For now, I will leave my conversation with postmodern persons for another time and address the former group, who may be offended by my beliefs.

As I understand it, the basic argument from the exclusivist perspective is holding the New Testament as the revealed Word of God and taking seriously what it says. In chapter nine, I considered John 14:6 and Acts 4:12. Other relevant texts affirm that only Jesus saves (see 1 Corinthians 3:11, 1 Timothy 2:5, 1 John 5:12). The New Testament also teaches that humanity is lost without Jesus Christ (Romans 1:21; 3:9). Further still, the New Testament contains texts that call on persons to hear and believe the gospel about Jesus in order to be saved (John 3:36). No matter where our respective journeys go, we need to acknowledge and engage these Bible passages.

I hold to these passages when I meet those who are inquiring what the Christian faith offers in their search for peace within and peace with God. At the same time, in our interreligious world, where many are deeply formed and guided by other religious perspectives, I believe there is room in God's grace for them as well.

Persons holding the exclusivist view would answer that conversion, and not just conversation, is the desired outcome. When asked if revelation occurred in other religions, more questions would need to be explored. As to whether dialogue between religions is possible, some would say yes and others no. But whether or not salvation is possible for those in other religions, exclusivists would say not.

How then can exclusivist and inclusivist Christians relate to each other in a way worthy of the gospel that claims us both? We might start with what Christian fellowship and community has been at its best:

• We affirm our love for and faith in Jesus Christ, who binds us together as Christians.

• We commit to strengthening the Christian church, the body of Christ, into which we have been called.

• We see each other as sisters and brothers whom Christ loves and for whom he died.

• We share a desire for Jesus and for Christians to be seen in the best possible light by persons of other faiths and those who have no faith.

I was touched by an article by Nabeel Jabbour, who is an expert on Muslim culture and would describe himself as an exclusivist. He wrote, "I used to think that successful evangelism was leading someone to Christ. I gave up on that definition long ago; its shortcomings became especially clear when God put Muslims on my heart. Instead I understand successful evangelism to mean helping every unchurched person I am in contact with to move one little step closer to Christ."[7]

This is where Christians of differing opinions can converge: in the hope that our life, witness, and relationships will be a means of persons seeing our Lord and our faith community in a more positive light. And then, out of celebrating our faith we share, we Christians can also acknowledge we have some differences on an important subject, differences that we can manage, discuss, and perhaps go different ways in our approaches and strategies.

In this spirit, I am aware of a number of criticisms that exist regarding the thoughts and information I have presented in this book. My descriptions might be seen as simplistic and naïve. Some may feel that I have ignored the troubling observations of certain scholars regarding Muhammad, about his several marriages after the death of his first wife, about some of the militarism in portions of the Qur'an and Hadith. Some may think that I have not paid enough attention to violent acts and movements in which the perpetrators say they have acted in the name of Allah and Islam. And others may point out that I have not dwelt upon the intolerance and restriction on other religions in some Muslim majority nations.

I acknowledge that there are many other things I could have said. I have chosen to focus on the opportunities for dialogue and mutual exchange in the North-American setting among peace-loving Christians, Jews, and Muslims. Some of these hard questions will need to be explored at a time in the future as these conversations grow deeper.

I know that my Christian friends who don't share my current positions on these topics may call on me to be more realistic in some of my descriptions. I in turn may want to ask them not to believe all the negative things they hear but to do some in-depth study about these three Abrahamic religions. As we have earlier noted, Todd Green has spoken of "professional Islamophobists," and unfortunately a few of those are well-known religious leaders in our country. Sometimes Christian people who share these religious leaders' views on other matters accept too readily the hateful things they say about Islam. I caution against blanket condemnations of a religious leader or a religion.

These differences among us Christians will not go away easily. Perhaps what we need is "conflict transformation." In conflict transformation, the goal is not so much to resolve an issue but rather to experience two things: empowerment and recognition. The first term means empowerment of self (in regards to goals, options, skills, resources and more), and the second refers to recognition of the other (in thought, words, actions). Christian mediators point out that in conflict transformation we live out our Lord's command to love our neighbors as ourselves. In empowerment, I love myself as I listen carefully to my heart, my feelings, hopes, needs, values, and commitments. In recognition, I obey Jesus' command to love my neighbors. I listen as carefully to the heart, the dignity, and the worth of a brother or sister made in God's image as I do my own. Mediators have noted that when empowerment and recognition occur, the experience is so powerful and significant that settling the conflicted issue at hand becomes secondary.

I once had such an experience with a Christian brother on a topic that divides Christians. At the time, I was pastor in a western university community and received a letter addressed to all pastors from John, the director of the local prolife organization. The letter was an invitation to come preview a new prolife film that would be available to churches. A stamped postcard was enclosed for responding. I thought he deserved an answer, so I wrote that I was of a different opinion on this subject and also had something already scheduled on the date he mentioned. But, I added, if they showed the film at another time, I would come see it.

I thought that would be the end of it, but a few days later, I received a phone call from John. "Thanks for your card, he said. "I have the movie. If you have a projector, I will come over at a suitable time, and we can view and discuss it together." We found a mutually available time. When he arrived, we greeted each other cordially but stiffly, sat down, and watched the movie together.

When it finished, he asked me, "Well, what did you think?" At first I attacked the cheap propaganda shots I thought it took. He responded, "Yeah, I know. But what did you think?" This led to a deep conversation as we each talked about what we believed, what experiences had led us to this, and where we felt uncomfortable with our positions. We also shared how we both longed for the day when abortion services were less needed and less of an issue. After rewinding the movie, we said our goodbyes.

John had the kindness to write me a note. I wish I still had it, but I can quote it almost word for word. He thanked me for taking the time to see the movie and discuss it. He went on, "I didn't convince you of my position, and I didn't expect to. You didn't convince me of your position, and I did not expect you to. But you took me more seriously than some people who agree with me, and for that I thank you." Though I haven't entirely changed my view, out of that experience I now think differently about the issue and the people who differ with me.

Recognition and empowerment. Conflict transformation. Holy ground. I hope for these things as we Christians live out our convictions on the complicated issues we face in an interreligious world.[8]

Reflect, Discuss, Do

1. Who are the persons with whom you can talk or disagree about anything? How did you get to that place?

2. Who are your closest spiritual friends with whom you can share convictions and discuss differences? How did you get to that place?

3. How well does your church do in addressing differences? What do you do well? What more do you hope for?

4. Where do you find yourself in the differences on interfaith matters explored in this chapter? Have you stated what you believe to anyone else? Where would be a safe place to do so?

5. Have you ever experienced conflict transformation? Tell another about your experience and the significance of recognition and empowerment.

6. **Do:** Reach out to someone with whom you differ on these topics and try to understand each other, what you believe, and why.

Notes

1. Dennis Hollinger, *Choosing the Good: Christian Ethics in a Complex World* (Grand Rapids: Baker Academic, 2002), 152, as cited in Richard P. Olson, *Love Letter to a Conflicted Church: Promise in Our Anger and Disagreements* (Eugene, OR: Wipf and Stock, 2010), 78.

2. I am quoting myself in *Love Letter to a Conflicted Church* (Eugene, OR: Wipf and Stock, 2010), 78. Chapter 5 is a more detailed discussion of the conflicts Christians have on interpreting Scripture.

3. Debra Bendis, "No Longer Strangers," *The Christian Century*, March 19, 2014, 22. http://www.swiaf.org/wp-content/uploads/2014/05/1403-No-Longer-Strangers-The-Christian-Century.pdf.

4. Ibid., 23.

5. Ibid.

6. Larry Engel, "The Pastors of Richland County," *The Christian Century*, September 14, 2016, 34.

7. Nabeel T. Jabbour, as quoted in Evelyne A. Reisacher, *Joyful Witness in the Muslim World: Sharing the Gospel in Everyday Encounters* (Grand Rapids: Baker Academic, 2016), 72.

8. I have summarized the theories and information about conflict transformation in more detail in chapter 2 of my book *Love Letter to a Conflicted Church* (Eugene, OR: Wipf and Stock, 2010), 21–31.

CHAPTER TWELVE

Where Does This Lead Us?

When Christiane Amanpour asked . . . , "What do you think are the key, pressing spiritual issues of our time?" my answer was quick and clear. I said, "The role religion is going to play in the 21st century is going to be one of the key issues. Faith can either be a barrier of division, a bomb of destruction, or a bridge of cooperation. Our job is to make it a bridge of cooperation." —Eboo Patel[1]

Bridges are the lifelines of a society on the move. They enable us to cross the deepest gorges and widest rivers, linking the two sides with a flow of traffic.—Diana Eck[2]

In 2011, at a time when it seemed that interfaith relations, especially Christian-Muslim relations, were at a low ebb, I was touched by a story in *Sojourners* magazine. Pastor Steve Stone of Heartsong Church (United Methodist) in suburban Memphis learned that a local mosque had bought property right across the street from his church. He decided to put up a sign, "Heartsong Church welcomes Memphis Islamic Center to the neighborhood." Though the Muslim group was hoping to slip in quietly and escape attention, they appreciated this gesture and contacted the pastor to ask if they could meet. *Sojourners* writer Bob Smietana relates,

That small act of kindness was the start of an unlikely friendship between the two congregations, one that made headlines around the world. Members of the mosque and church have shared meals together, worked [together] at a homeless shelter, and become friends over the past two years. When [the pastor] learned that his Muslim friends needed a place to pray for Ramadan because their building wasn't ready, he opened up the doors of the church and let them hold their prayers [in the worship space of his church].[3]

This act of hospitality outraged some Heartsong members—about twenty left. Critics said Pastor Stone was a heretic for allowing these people to pray in the church. For the most part, however, the church's welcome had a positive response around Memphis. "He says he's just doing what Jesus taught him to do. 'Jesus told us to love our neighbors,' Stone told [the press]. These people are actually neighbors.'"[4] This story was also told around the world:

A group of Muslims in a small town in Kashmir, the disputed region near the border of India and Pakistan with much Muslim-Christian tension, saw a report on CNN [about this church's hospitality]. "God has spoken to us through this man," they said. Another added, "How can we kill these people?" A third man went straight to the local Christian church and cleaned it inside and out. These Muslims sent a message to Pastor Stone. "We are now trying to be good neighbors, too. Tell your congregation we do not hate them, we love them, and for the rest of our lives we are going to take care of that little church."[5]

This occurred at about same time that a Florida pastor was also gaining worldwide attention by threatening to burn Qur'ans (a great sacrilege and offense, as we have noted) as a means of supposedly bargaining that the Islamic Center near Ground Zero in Manhattan not be built. As a lover of Christ and the church, I am so grateful to Pastor Steve Stone and Heartsong for demonstrating that we Christians can be, and are for the most part, loving and hospitable people.

I have since discovered more stories of such friendship and trust than I had thought existed. When a growing group of Muslims was looking for a place in the northern part of Kansas City large enough for them to meet, they inquired at Hillside Christian Church. The pastor invited their leaders to meet with the church board. During that meeting, the Muslim group was asked what their opinion of Jesus was. Shahzad Shaifique recalls, "We told them as Muslims, we believe in all of the prophets, including Jesus. It is a part of our faith. They said if we had that kind of belief in Jesus, we were more than welcome to come and use the facility."[6]

Persons of goodwill are leading the way and providing examples for us in this quest for positive Christian-Muslim relationships. As I conclude my conversation with you in this book about trying to be Christlike in an interreligious world, we have a few more things to explore.

God calls us as Christ-followers both *to do* and *to be*. I believe that out of the ferment of these times, God is calling to us as disciples of Christ to do (at least) the following:

• To become more deeply involved in friendship, conversation, and dialogue with persons of other faiths where we live and work.

• To be aware, supportive, and proactive when negativity, threats, and attacks happen to persons and places of worship of other faiths.

• To be compassionate and active in responding to the worldwide refugee crisis, including at the local level.

• To offer understanding, care, and support to the vastly growing number of interfaith marriages and families.

Called to Do: Build Relationships

Sociologists Robert D. Putnam and David E. Campbell investigate a lovely puzzle in their book *American Grace*. It may be stated this way: "Unique among nations, America is deeply religious, religiously diverse, and remarkably tolerant."[7] In recent years the nation's religious landscape has changed, with more tension and polarization between those on the religious right and those on the religious left. Still, amazingly, our attacks and violence against each other have been minimal when compared to other places in the world with diverse populations.

What accounts for this happy truth? Putnam and Campbell urge us not to "miss the forest for the trees," which is that "*most Americans are intimately acquainted with people of other faiths*. This, we argue, is the most important reason that Americans can combine religious devotion with diversity."[8] They playfully illustrate this theory with what they call the "Aunt Susan Principle." Virtually every family has an "Aunt Susan"—a member of the extended family whose religion is different from the rest but who personifies that religion to the family and thus influences their attitudes. Whoever our Aunt Susan is, "having a religiously diverse social network leads to more positive assessment of specific religious groups."[9]

Again and again, the authors find that when Americans associate with people of religions other than their own, they become more accepting of that other religion. Gradually, we move from religious tolerance to a celebration of diversity for its own sake.

In their final paragraph, Putnam and Campbell ask and answer the basic question of their study: "How has America solved the puzzle of religious pluralism—the coexistence of religious diversity and devotion? And how has it done so in the wake of growing religious polarization? By creating a web of interlocking personal relationships among people of many different faiths. This is America's grace."[10]

The common-sense takeaway from their study is simply to be fully part of your personal world. Get to know coworkers, neighbors, and parents of your children's friends. In nonthreatening ways, be transparent about your religious life and openly curious about theirs. When some of these overtures evolve into deeper relationships, it can be an occasion for growth for both of you.

It has been frequently noted that we will have no peace in the world without peace among the religions. And we will have no peace among religions without dialogue between persons in those religions. As Putnam and Campbell remind us, we Americans are in an ideal and logical place for these sorts of dialogues to happen. True, this is a small part of what our world needs, but it is vitally important and an aspect of our calling to be Christlike wherever we are. I hope that you be led to seek deeper conversations to learn and understand more thoroughly what you hold in common with those of another religion and where you differ.

In the wake of the 9/11 attacks, Ranya Idliby, a Muslim, reached out to find two mothers—a Christian and a Jew—with the hope that they could together write a children's book about their common heritage. Suzanne Oliver, a Christian, and Priscilla Warner, a Jew, responded to her invitation. As they became acquainted and started to conceptualize this children's book, they came to realize that they had much to do as adults to articulate their own faith journeys, explore the questions and issues they had with the others' faith, and learn how to relate together through these differences. The conversations proceeded, growing in depth and participating in each other's religious observances and holidays. In time, as they persisted, not only more basic understanding but deep friendships developed. Eventually, they wrote about this journey. It is called *The Faith Club: A Muslim, A Christian, A Jew—Three Women Search for Understanding.*[11] The book also has appendices on "How to Start a Faith Club" and "More Faith Club Questions."

There are many doorways and resources for such interfaith explorations. We can take advantage of this "American Grace" of religious diversity in our workplaces, neighborhoods, and schools. Talking, listening, and working together, we can make these safe and hospitable places for all.

Called to Do: Supportiveness after Threats or Attacks

Sadly, despite our efforts to build goodwill, we will still have hate groups and individuals who vandalize places of worship and threaten, injure, or kill individuals whom they view as different or a threat.

As I was beginning this chapter, one of those harsh and terrible attacks almost happened in Garden City, a community of about twenty-five-thousand people located in Finney County in western Kansas. Up to the time of the thwarted attack, this area seemed to be one of the success stories of an increasingly diverse America. Some forty-thousand people live in Finney County. Forty-six percent are of white European descent, while the other 54 percent are of various other descents. The county's demographic has changed considerably in the last decade, with thirty-five languages and dialects, in addition to English, now spoken in the schools. Persons from ten different African countries, as well as Burmese and Mexicans, are among the new residents. Somalis had been invited to spend Thanksgiving and other holidays in the houses of lifelong Garden City families, and in turn they welcomed their non-Somali neighbors over for Muslim holidays. In Garden City you will find a small, makeshift mosque as well as a Buddhist prayer room, plus churches with Christians from various nationalities. Many of these new residents came for the well-paying, entry-level jobs in the county's meat-packing plants.

Despite some minor tensions, the growing city had remained, for the most part, peaceful. This peace was threatened by three men—Kansans with anti-government, anti-Muslim, and anti-immigrant extremist beliefs. They called themselves "Crusaders" and their intended targets "cockroaches." In October 2016 they were arrested for planning to detonate trucks full of explosives outside an apartment complex housing mostly Somali families.

A newspaper article describes the longer-term white residents as horrified and embarrassed. Benjamin Anderson commented, "Lovely people, the Somalis and all the other people who live among us." John Doll added, "This is terrible, because these people they targeted are great people; they work hard, pay taxes, obey the laws. Why would anyone want to hurt them?" Father Reginald Urban noted, "This will bring fear into the homes of many people. But it won't change how accepting this community is of people from all languages, theologies and philosophies."[12] Community leaders, FBI investigators, and local police tried to reassure residents and bring calm as the community reached out with support and vigils.

When such threats and attacks come to our neighbors, what is our calling as Christians? Ed Chasteen, a retired professor of William Jewell College in Liberty Missouri, has led an informal organization of students called "Hatebusters." For nearly thirty years, they have tried to live out their calling in just such times as I have described. When an attack (or threat of an attack) or vandalism occurs to an individual, a home, or a place of worship, Ed and his group spring into action. He notifies his network and invites letters of support to the threatened or attacked person or group, which he takes to the victims and inquires what more people of goodwill can do to help. For example, recently the partially constructed mosque in the northland of Kansas City was the target of vandalism and an attempted fire, fortunately mostly unsuccessful. Here is part of Ed's blog about Hatebusters' caring response:

> The recent fire caused little damage. It did cause fear: that others might do them harm; that no one might care. Our breakfast is our beginning effort to allay their fears and send a message that such mistreatment of our neighbors is not welcome and will not be tolerated. Ann Henning will call Laeeq's wife to find out how she and others from our church might help. Jeff will contact Khalid to plan how students from our college can help with tree plantings planned for the property where the mosque is being built.[13]

This group is acting on a calling that is for all of us—not just to build relationships but also to respond to hate, disrespect, vandalism, and attacks. We can assure victims that such attacks are not welcomed and that people of goodwill desire a just and accepting community.

When I inquired of friends at two other Islamic centers, they told me that they had occasional graffiti or other defacement at their places of worship and occasional threatening phone calls. When these events happened, they received supportive calls from Jewish and Christian friends, expressing support and offering to help.

We all need to be aware and responsive to Islamophobia and anti-Semitism wherever we encounter it—in everyday conversations, in the news media, where we live and work. Being Christlike calls for an informed, loving peace with justice.

Called to Do: Advocacy and Involvement with Refugees

It is well-known that we have a world refugee crisis, with literally millions of Syrians having left their tragically war-torn and dangerous homeland. Nearby countries are overwhelmed. One in six people in Lebanon are now refugees. In Jordan, the biggest refugee camp has become that nation's fourth-largest city. European nations have absorbed thousands upon thousands of refugees. A few of those refugees have inflicted harm, which complicates the willingness to respond to this humanitarian crisis.

American policy and practice in offering a modest response to this need has been restricted and delayed. Some of our state governments have refused to allow refugees to enter, stating fear of terrorists. All of this calls for compassionate Christian awareness and response. Americans need to know that our country has a long, complicated vetting process for any refugees who want to come to the United States. It starts with a screening by the United Nations High Commissioner for Refugees. The months-long process approves about one percent of the applicants.

If a refugee passes this evaluation, next comes a "security clearance check that could take several rounds, an in-person interview, approval by the Department of Homeland Security, medical screening, a match with a sponsor agency, 'cultural orientation' classes, and one final security clearance."[14] This series of steps takes an average of two years. The process for a refugee to be accepted is the most extensive security screening that our government does.

In the light of this detailed process, a few things become clear for us who are trying to be Christlike. First, any acceptance of refugees is a miniscule part of the needed response to this vast problem. Further, all reasonable steps will have been taken to assure that refugees received are fleeing terrorism—and are not terrorists. Further still, we are called to be Christian citizens advocating for these refugees and challenging political leaders who reject them. If we believe in the mandate to live by the "Golden Rule" (Matthew 7:12) and to welcome strangers (Matthew 25:31-40) we will be responsive and helpful, on whatever level we can, to the refugees who are finally allowed to come to our communities.

This involvement can take many forms and levels. In my community, a refugee advocacy organization offers this list of ways to be helpful: donate household goods and furniture; visit refugee families with friendship and offers of help; help set up houses for newly arriving persons; help with English as a Second Language classes; if you have language skills, offer translation help; join an airport welcoming team; create hygiene packs; organize a welcome picnic; spread the word. Perhaps your congregation might consider sponsoring a refugee family.

Called to Do: Care and Support for Interfaith Marriages and Families

Sociologists and authors Putnam and Campbell point out that approximately half of all US residents marry someone who is from a different religious tradition and that about a third of all marriages today are mixed (because, for some, one partner or the other adopts the other's religious practices).[15] That figure may seem unbelievably high until we learn what they mean by "religious tradition." Up to now we have been speaking broadly of the religious traditions of Christians, Muslims, and Jews. Putnam and Campbell's categories are different. The varied traditions—with distinctive beliefs, practices, and relationships—that they identify are these: Evangelical Protestant, Mainline Protestant, Black Protestant, Catholic, Mormon, Jew, other faiths (which includes Muslims), and none. Seen from that perspective, it becomes more believable that half of marriages are between persons from different traditions. This percentage of intermarriages has grown from under 30 percent to more than 50 percent over the last century. Resistance and restrictions on such marriages—by families or religious authorities—have been relaxed over that same time.

These marriages constitute a challenge and an opportunity for the couples. The challenge is how to maintain practices, convictions, and rituals that each finds significant and still share a spiritual journey with a spouse. The opportunity is to learn from each other, from participation in each other's faith practices, family, and community, and, perhaps, to create something new.

In her book *Being Both: Embracing Two Religions in One Interfaith Family*, Susan Katz Miller describes and advocates for interfaith marriages in that broader sense of crossing major religious borders. Starting with her own marriage, she mostly speaks of Jewish-Christian marriages but also gives attention to Muslims, Hindus, and Buddhists.

Religious intermarriage is discouraged by most Jewish institutions and many Christian denominations. To this day Orthodox and Conservative Jewish rabbis will not officiate at an interfaith marriage. Some Jewish leaders call intermarriage the "silent Holocaust." And yet intermarriage grows; indeed, the rate for Jews choosing to intermarry was calculated to be 47 percent by the turn of the twenty-first century.[16]

Miller describes a growing grassroots movement of interfaith couples seeking mutual support and resources in embracing both faiths for themselves and their children. Here are the benefits of dual-faith marriage as she sees them: promoting transparency about differences; encouraging extended family unity; sidestepping the matrilineality conflict (the debate within Judaism as to whether Jewishness comes through only the mother); providing literacy in both religions; and providing cultural harmony.[17] These dual-faith marriages, Miller believes, are a gift to the world. "As interfaith children, born with the potential to walk in more than one pair of religious shoes or to see through more than one religious lens, we have a unique role to play in reducing religious intolerance and promoting religious peace."[18]

As she reflects on her own journey, Miller notes that, aware of her husband's rich Christian heritage and her beloved Judaism, she had no choice but to raise their children interfaith. "But I did not anticipate how choosing both would create *joy*, and not simply compromise in our lives. My husband and I have reveled in the pleasure of our intellectual interfaith collaboration and lovingly shared our traditions with each other and with our children. We have been able to sit together as a family in a church pew, in a synagogue, and in our interfaith families community, feeling intensely fulfilled in each environment."[19]

Large urban areas may have communities and organizations specifically for interfaith couples. Whether that is available or not, all of us seeking to be Christlike are called to offer understanding, interest, support, and church flexibility for those in interreligious marriages and families. This is a rapidly growing grassroots movement in spite of much religious opposition and indifference. It is time to extend Christian love and graces to these families.

Called to Be: The Impact on My Faith Journey and Yours

My focus now changes from what we are called to *do* to what we are called to *be*. I need to ask myself what the God of history is whispering to me, both out of the story of our times and out of the personal journeys, studies, and encounters I have been sharing with you. You have a similar question to ask out of your journey and encounters (including with me in this book and the ventures I have encouraged you to take).

What has happened to me and within me as I have walked this road? Have I experienced spiritual discoveries and insights from sources outside my Christian faith? Have I encountered saints, holy persons, who are other than Christian? Have I experienced revelations from God? If I answer yes to any of these, what change has this made in me?

Out of her much more extensive studies, author Diana Eck faced these questions. She describes herself as a "Christian, a Montana-born, lifelong Methodist." She has studied Hindu and other traditions in India and was the director of the extensive Harvard-based "Pluralism Project" that explored religious change in America. In what ways does she articulate her faith in the light of her wide-ranging exploration of other religions? She responds, "Through the years I have found my own faith not threatened, but broadened and deepened by the study of Hindu, Buddhist, Muslim, and Sikh traditions of faith." This has led to deeper awareness and desire "to be faithful to the mystery and presence of the one I call God."[20] How is this true? She responds, "Being a Christian pluralist means daring to encounter people of very different faith traditions and defining my faith not by its borders, but by its roots."[21]

I am a Christian, South Dakota-born, lifelong American Baptist. I have been on the "beginners trail" of the same journey and am arriving at similar conclusions. My thinking is stimulated by the discovery of the discussion already underway of "multiple religious participation." Here is professor of comparative theology John Berthrong's definition of this term: "Multiple religious participation is the conscious (and sometimes unconscious) use of religious ideas, practices, symbols, meditations, prayers, chants, and sensibilities derived from one tradition by a member of another community of faith for their own purposes."[22] Many practices of other religions are now part of our culture and we likely engage in them unconscious of their religious roots.

As I read the book *Many Yet One? Multiple Religious Belonging*,[23] I became aware that I had adopted a practice that originated in another religion without even realizing it. As a pastoral counselor, I studied and adopted Herbert Benson's "Relaxation Response"—slow, deep, relaxed, meditative breathing, as with each breath one silently repeats a word or phrase. Mine is usually from my Christian faith: *peace* or *Jesus* or *God is love*. Benson's research has discovered the Relaxation Response to be a helpful way to address a number of maladies including high blood pressure (one of my health issues). Benson adapted his Relaxation Response from the practice of Transcendental Meditation, which was in turn a simplification and popularizing of classic Buddhist and Hindu meditation methods. It's also very similar to the Jesus Prayer of Eastern Orthodox Christianity and the Centering Prayer of Western monastic traditions. These practices not only from Christianity but also from other religions have enriched my life and improved my health.

At the same time, my journey has not been so much about diverse practices as it has been a journey of the mind and heart. This began with meeting and getting to know persons from other religions—persons I came to enjoy, admire, and love. Each of them responded to inquiries and helped even when it inconvenienced them to do so. Their hospitality, self-giving, and openness to sharing what their faith meant to them without pressuring me to convert touched me deeply. I realize I have met the finest, and that each religion has its problems and problem people. But I am grateful for the open door I have experienced.

Their communities have also touched me. When I worship with Muslim or Jewish people, I don't participate very much; I mostly observe. I am touched by an atmosphere of devotion, faith, and desire to be obedient to God. The languages that I do not understand, and the rituals and music with which I am unfamiliar, nonetheless stir my awareness of the otherness and greatness of God. The warm greetings, conversations, and hospitality before and after the worship experience remind me of our common humanity despite our religious differences.

And when I study the story of each religion's founder and of that religion's growth and development, I discern in them, as in mine, God's revelation to a person in response to the need of a people. The development of the religion has its good and evil within it, as does mine. My faith is enhanced, not diminished, by the belief that God has addressed persons in other times and places to draw them to faith in God and to do justice under God.

Almost every Sunday morning, I worship at the Baptist church where I have been a member for the last thirty years. I love to be with those people, my family with whom we have shared so much over the years. As the seasons of the church year roll by, I welcome the retelling of the story of the One who is my Savior, my inspiration, my guide. But once in a while, I wish we would also speak of this wider human family of believers of which we are also a part.

On a recent Sunday, this thought came to me as we were singing a favorite, "In Christ There Is No East or West." A few alternate words came to mind. I could not let it go until, weeks later, I had written the kind of hymn I sometimes long for. As we bid each other farewell and offer each other God's blessings, sing it along with me, if you wish.

Faith Calls from Us
Faith calls from us a broader view
Than we have had before.
We live within a shrinking world.
We've less trust but need more.

We're sisters, brothers, partners all,
What faith that each may claim.
We serve and pray in varied ways
With hopes and fears the same.

Allah, Yahweh, and mother God,
Those varied words mean one.
One creator of us all—
This vision's but begun.

But we who came from Abraham
Have gone our separate ways.
We have misunderstood and fought.
Forgive our foolish ways.

Each faith has reason to repent.
We've those who fail to see
Your teaching and just plan for us,
But act so violently.

Much more than half of humankind
Are Muslim, Christian, Jew.
The peace of the entire world
Awaits a broader view.
Shalom, salaam, and peace to all,
Oh, let us see Your face
In each and all these varied paths,
Your rainbow human race.

Reflect, Discuss, Do

1. This chapter speaks of four areas where we are called to *do* to get involved: deeper involvement in interfaith conversations; support in the face of threat or attack; welcome of refugees; and support of interfaith marriages.

a. In which of these is your church already involved?

b. In which of these are you personally involved?

c. Where do you sense a call to become more involved? What might be your first step?

2. The chapter also explores a call to be/become—that is, to consider change in one's spiritual-theological journey and perspective. What have you experienced in these conversations? Was it upsetting or enriching or both? Tell another about your journey.

3. **Do:** Continue to learn more about another religion. When I asked a leader in a local mosque where to start in learning more about Islam, he suggested the website https://www.whyislam.org/. To learn more about Judaism, you might start with Rabbi Lawrence Kushner's lovely book, *Jewish Spirituality: A Brief Introduction for Christians.*

Notes

1. Eboo Patel, "What is the key spiritual issue of our time?" on Interfaith Youth Core Website, April 25, 2011, accessed November 2, 2016, https://www.ifyc.org/content/what-key-spiritual-issue-our-time.

2. Diana L. Eck, *A New Religious America: How a "Christian Country" Has Become the World's Most Religiously Diverse Nation* (New York: HarperSanFrancisco, 2001), 335.

3. Bob Smietana, "Peace Be Upon Them," *Sojourners*, September–October, 2011, 16.

4. Ibid.

5. Ibid., 5.

6. Karen Ridder, "KC area Muslims seek to educate people on their religion to promote better understanding, The Kansas City Star, August 3, 2016, 17JO.

7. Robert D. Putnam and David E. Campbell. *American Grace: How Religion Divides and Unites Us* (New York: Simon and Schuster, 2010), front flap.

8. Ibid., 526.

9. Ibid., 526–527.

10. Ibid., 550.

11. Ranya Idliby, Suzanne Oliver, and Priscilla Warner, *The Faith Club: A Muslim, A Christian, A Jew—Three Women Search for Understanding* (New York: Free Press, 2006). They also have a website with other suggestions and resources at https://www.thefaith club.com/.

12. Roy Wenzl, "Community 'devasted' after terrorist plot announcements, arrests," The Kansas City Star, October 15, 2016, 2A.

13. Ed Chasteen, Hatebusters website, accessed November 23, 2016, http://hatebusters.com/blog.htm.

14. "Here's What the U.S. Process for Vetting Syrian Refugees Actually Looks Like," The Week website, November 16, 2015, accessed November 27, 2016, http://theweek.com/speedreads/589290/heres-what-process-vetting-syrian-refugees-actually-looks-like.

15. Putnam and Campbell, *American Grace*, 148–149.

16. Susan Katz Miller, *Being Both: Embracing Two Religions in One Interfaith Family* (Boston: Beacon Press, 2013), xiii.

17. Ibid., 20–53.

18. Ibid., 224.

19. Ibid., 225.

20. Eck, *New Religious America*, 23.

21. Ibid.

22. John Berthrong, *The Divine Deli: Religious Identity in the North American Cultural Mosaic* (Maryknoll, NY: Orbis Books, 1999), 35.

23. Peniel Jesudason Rufus Rajkumar and Joseph Prabhakar Dayam, eds., *Many Yet One? Multiple Religious Belong* (Geneva: World Council of Churches Publications, 2016).

BIBLIOGRAPHY

Allen, Roger and Shawkat M. Toorawa, eds. *Islam: A Short Guide to the Faith*. Grand Rapids: William B. Eerdmans Publishing Company, 2011.

Araujo-Hawkins, Dawn. "A Jew, a Christian, and a Muslim walk into a parking lot...." *Sojourners* 45, no. 6, (June, 2016): 28-31.

Bendis, Debra. "No Longer Strangers." *The Christian Century*, March 19, 2014.

Bennett, Clinton. *Understanding Christian-Muslim Relations, Past and Present*. New York: Continuum, 2008.

Denny, Frederick M. "Islam and Ecology: A Bestowed Trust Inviting Balanced Stewardship." Yale University. The Forum on Religion and Ecology at Yale. Undated. Accessed August 1, 2016. http://fore.yale.edu/religion/islam.

Dirks, Jerald F. *The Abrahamic Faiths: Judaism, Christianity and Islam Similarities and Contrasts*. Beltsville, MD: Amana Publications, 2004.

Eck, Diana L. *A New Religious America: How a "Christian Country" Has Become the World's Most Religiously Diverse Nation*. New York: HarperSanFrancisco, 2001.

Engel, Larry. "The Pastors of Richland County." *The Christian Century*, September 14, 2016.

Epstein, Greg M. *Good without God: What a Billion Nonreligious People Do Believe*. New York: William Morrow, 2009.

Esposito, John L. *Great World Religions: Islam*. Chantilly, VA: The Teaching Company Limited Partnership, 2003.

_____. *Islam: The Straight Path*. Fourth Edition. New York: Oxford University Press,

_____. *What Everyone Needs to Know About Islam*. Oxford: Oxford University Press, 2002.

Fox, Matthew. *One River, Many Wells: Wisdom Springing from Global Faiths*. New York: Jeremy P. Tarcher/Penguin, 2004.

Fuller, Millard. *The Theology of the Hammer*. Macon, GA: Smyth & Helwys Publishing, Inc., 1994.

Gerges, Fawaz A. *ISIS: A History*. Princeton: Princeton University Press, 2016.

Goldman, Shalom. *Jewish-Christian Difference and Modern Jewish Identity: Seven Twentieth-Century Converts*. Landham, MD: Lexington Books, 2015.

Green, Todd. *The Fear of Islam: An Introduction to Islamophobia in the West*. Minneapolis: Fortress Press, 2015.

Gushee, David P. "Learning from the Christian Rescuers: Lessons for the Churches." *The Annals of the American Academy of Political and Social Science*. 548 (1996): 138–155, Accessed August 12, 2016, http://www.jstor.org/stable/1048549.

Haynes, Stephen R. "Changing Paradigms: Reformist, Radical and Rejectionist Approaches to the Relationship between Christianity and Anti-semitism," *Journal of Ecumenical Studies* 32, No. 1 (Winter 1995): 63–88.

Heim, S. Mark. *Salvations: Truth and Difference in Religion*. Maryknoll: Orbis Books, 1995.

Helminski, Kabir Edmund. *A Living Presence: A Sufi Way to Mindfulness and the Essential Self*. Threshold Books/Jeremy Tarcher, 1992; The Threshold Society. 2016. Accessed August 23, 2016. http://sufism.org/lineage/sufism.

Hendi, Imam Yahya. "The Story of Abraham: A journey of hope for all." College of St. Elizabeth. July 19, 2003. Accessed November 21, 2017. http://imamyahyahendi.com/library_articles_2.htm.

Bibliography

Hollinger, Dennis. *Choosing the Good: Christian Ethics in a Complex World*. Grand Rapids: Baker Academic, 2002.

Idilby, Ranya, Suzanne Oliver, and Priscilla Warner. *The Faith Club: A Muslim, A Christian, A Jew—Three Women Search for Understanding*. New York: Free Press, 2006.

Jesudason, Peniel, Rufus Rajkumar and Joseph Prabhakar Dayam, eds. *Many Yet One? Multiple Religious Belonging*. Geneva: World Council of Churches Publications, 2016.

Jones, Robert P. *The End of White Christian America*. New York: Simon and Schuster, 2016.

Kateregga, Badru D., and David W. Shenk. *A Muslim and a Christian in Dialogue*. Scottdale, PA: Herald Press, 1997.

Khalidi, Tarif, ed., and trans. *The Muslim Jesus: Sayings and Stories in Islamic Literature*. Cambridge: Harvard University Press, 2001.

Kimball, Charles. *Striving Together: A Way Forward in Christian-Muslim Relations*. Maryknoll, NY: Orbis Books, 1991.

_____. *When Religion Becomes Evil*. New York: HarperSanFrancisco, 2001.

_____. *When Religion Becomes Lethal: The Explosive Mix of Politics and Religion in Judaism, Christianity, and Islam*. San Francisco: Jossey-Bass, 2011.

King, Ursula. "Christian Mystics Explained." 1999–2014. Accessed August 28, 2016. http://www.christianmystics.com/basics/ whatis.html.

Knitter, Paul F. *Introducing Theologies of Religion*. Maryknoll: Orbis Books, 2002.

_____. *Without Buddha I Could Not Be a Christian*. Oxford: One World Publications, 2009.

Kushner, Lawrence. *Jewish Spirituality: A Brief Introduction for Christians*. Woodstock, VT: Jewish Lights Publishing, 2001, 2002.

_____. *Kabbalah: A Love Story*. New York: Morgan Road Books, 2006.

Küng, Hans, Josef van Ess, Heinrich von Stietencron, and Heinz Bechert. Translated by Peter Heinegg. *Christianity & World Religions: Paths to Dialogue*. Maryknoll: Orbis Books, English translation 1986, 1993, third printing 1997.

LaFantasie, Glenn W., ed. *The Correspondence of Roger Williams, Volume II: 1654–1682*. Providence and London: Brown University Press/University Press of New England, 1988. Accessed January 4, 2016. http://www.worldpolicy.org/sites/default/files/uploaded/image/Williams-1670-Forced%20worship%20stinks.pdf.
Levine, Amy. *The Misunderstood Jew: The Church and the Scandal of the Jewish Jesus*. New York: HarperOne, 2006.

Mercadante, Linda A. *Belief without Borders: Inside the Minds of the Spiritual but Not Religious*. New York: Oxford University Press, 2014.
Miller, Susan Katz. *Being Both: Embracing Two Religions in One Interfaith Family*. Boston: Beacon Press, 2013.

Norris, Kathleen. *Amazing Grace: A Vocabulary of Faith*. New York: Riverhead Books, 1998.

Olson, Richard P. *Love Letter to a Conflicted Church: Promise in Our Anger and Disagreements*. Eugene, Oregon: Wipf and Stock, 2010.

Patel, Eboo. *Acts of Faith: The Story of an American Muslim, the Struggle for the Soul of a Generation*. Boston, Beacon Press, 2007.
_____. *Sacred Ground: Pluralism, Prejudice, and the Promise of America*. Boston: Beacon Press, 2012.
_____. "What is the key spiritual issue of our time?" on Interfaith Youth Core Website, April 25, 2011. Accessed November 2, 2016. https://www.ifyc.org/content/what-key-spiritual-issue-our-time.
Prothero, Stephen. *God Is Not One: The Eight Rival Religions That Run the World—and Why Their Differences Matter*. New York: HarperOne, 2010.

Bibliography

Putnam, Robert D. and David E. Campbell. *American Grace: How Religion Divides and Unites Us*. New York: Simon and Schuster, 2010.

Qureshi, Nabeel. *Seeking Allah, Finding Jesus: A Devout Muslim Encounters Christianity*. Grand Rapids: Zondervan, 2014.

Rader, Lee L. "Fresh Winds in an Understanding of Pluralism." *The Journal of Pastoral Care* 51, no.1 (Spring 1997): 115-116.

Raybon, Patricia and Alana Raybon. *Undivided: A Muslim Daughter, Her Christian Mother, Their Path to Peace*. Nashville: W, Publishing Group of Thomas Nelson, 2015.

Reisacher, Evelyne A. *Joyful Witness in the Muslim World: Sharing the Gospel in Everyday Encounters*. Grand Rapids: BakerAcademic, 2016.

Royal Aal al-Bayt Institute for Islamic Thought, Jordan, "ACommonWord-Baptist-World-Alliance-Response.pdf," *The ACW Letter/A Common Word/Christian Responses*, December 28, 2008, accessed September 24, 2016, www.acommonword.com/category/site/christian-responses/.

Sarda, Ziauddin. *What Do Muslims Believe? The Roots and Realities of Modern Islam*. New York: Walker and Company, 2007.

Shah-Kazemi, Reza, trans. *My Mercy Encompasses All: The Koran's Teachings on Compassion, Peace and Love*. Berkeley: Counterpoint, 2007.

Shenk, David W. *Christian, Muslim, Friend.: Twelve Paths to Real Relationship*. Harrisonburg, VA: Herald Press, 2014.

Speight, R. Marshton. *God Is One: The Way of Islam*. New York: Friendship Press, 1989.

Stacey, Aisha. "Why Do Muslims Call Others to Islam?" August 18, 2014. Accessed July 17, 2016. http://www.islamreligion.com/articles/10655/why-do-muslims-call-others-to-islam/.

Stedman, Chris. *Faitheist: How an Atheist Found Common Ground with the Religious*. Boston: Beacon Press, 2012.

Steed, Brian L. *Bees and Spiders: Applied Cultural Awareness and the Art of Cross-Cultural Influence.* Houston: Strategic Book Publishing and Rights Co., 2014.

Tippett, Krista. *Becoming Wise: An Inquiry into the Mystery and Art of Living.* New York: Penguin Press, 2016.

Tzortzis, Hamza Andreas. "What Is Islamic Spirituality?" Undated. Accessed August 10, 2016. http://www.hamzatzortzis.com/1653/what-is-islamic-spirituality/.

United States Conference of Catholic Bishops. Second Vatican Council, Nostra Aetate 3. October 28, 1965. Accessed July 20, 2016. http://www.usccb.org/beliefs-and-teachings/ecumenical-and-interreligious/interreligious/islam/vatican-council-and-papal-statements-on-islam.cfm.

Volf, Miroslav. *Allah: A Christian Response.* New York: HarperOne, 2011.

Wiesel, Elie. *Night.* New York: Hill & Wang, 1960.

Wikipedia. "Zohar." Updated October 28, 2016. Accessed August 14, 2016. https://en.wikipedia.org/wiki/Zohar.

World Council of Churches. "Christian Witness in a Multi-Religious World." June 28, 2011. Accessed July 26, 2016. https://www.oikoumene.org/en/resources/documents/wcc-programmes/interreligious-dialogue-and-cooperation/christian-identity-in-pluralistic-societies/christian-witness-in-a-multi-religious-world.

_____. "Guidelines on Dialogue with People of Living Faiths and Ideologies." January 2, 2010. Accessed January 15, 2016. https://www.oikoumene.org/en/resources/documents/wcc-programmes/interreligious-dialogue-and-cooperation/interreligious-trust-and-respect/guidelines-on-dialogue-with-people-of-living-faiths-and-ideologies.

Zebiri, Kate. *Muslims and Christians Face to Face.* Oxford: One World, 1997.